Kenekuk, the Kickapoo Prophet

Kenekuk, the Kickapoo Prophet. George Catlin, who painted this portrait in 1831, called Kenekuk a "very shrewd and talented man" and the "champion of the mere remnant of a poisoned race," the Kickapoo Indians. Courtesy of the National Museum of American Art, Smithsonian Institution.

Kenekuk,
the Kickapoo Prophet

Joseph B. Herring

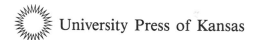 University Press of Kansas

© 1988 by the University Press of Kansas
All rights reserved

Published by the University Press of Kansas (Lawrence, Kansas
66045), which was organized by the Kansas Board of Regents and is
operated and funded by Emporia State University, Fort Hays State
University, Kansas State University, Pittsburg State University,
the University of Kansas, and Wichita State University

Library of Congress Cataloging-in-Publication Data

Herring, Joseph B., 1947–
  Kenekuk, the Kickapoo Prophet.
  Bibliography: p.
  Includes index.
  1. Kenekuk, Kickapoo Chief, ca. 1790–1852.
2. Kickapoo Indians—Biography. 3. Indians of North
America—Great Plains—History. 4. Potawatomi Indians—
Biography. 5. Kickapoo Indians—History. I. Title.
E99.K4K464 1988   978′.00497 [B]   88-206
ISBN 0-7006-0357-3

British Library Cataloguing in Publication Data is available.

Printed in the United States of America
10 9 8 7 6 5 4 3 2 1

The paper used in this publication meets the minimum requirements
of the American National Standard for Permanence of Paper for
Printed Library Materials Z39.48-1984.

In memory of
Walter Rundell, Jr.

Contents

Illustrations

Acknowledgments

This study could not have been possible without the assistance of many people. Special thanks must go to Donald Worcester and James Kettle, the best editors in the Southwest. Both men read the manuscript in its earlier stages and offered cogent criticisms and suggestions at every turn.

R. David Edmunds also deserves special mention. I learned much about American Indian history by reading Edmunds's books and attending his seminars at Texas Christian University. David is always ready to talk "Indians," and he has always answered my questions patiently and honestly. His advice on the techniques of research and writing Indian history have been invaluable. His high standards of excellence are equaled by few in the profession.

William E. Unrau of Wichita State University and Jeanne Cardenas of Kansas Newman College also read the manuscript and offered useful suggestions. I am grateful to them for the time spent helping to improve the manuscript.

Members of the history faculty at the University of Maryland also deserve credit. Horace Samuel Merrill, David Grimsted, Winthrop Wright, and Keith Olson taught me how to write and encouraged me to pursue the research on the Kickapoo Prophet. The late Walter Rundell, Jr., insisted that I quit my old job and enter the history profession. At his urging, I continued my graduate studies. Walter Rundell is the reason this project was undertaken and completed.

Research assistance and other help was provided by Kent Carter, Barbara Rust, Beverly Moody, Barbara Leahy, Overnice Wilks, Margie Jenkins, and Margaret Schmidt of the Federal Records Center at Fort Worth, Texas. Others who deserve credit include Darrell Garwood, Bob Knect, and Bobbie Pray of the Kansas State Historical Society; Alan Perry, Ann McFerrin, and Nancy Hulston of the Kansas City Federal Records Center; Margaret Harman of the Smithsonian Institution's National Museum of American Art; Joseph Forte, Sister Dolores Strunk, and Mary Richardet of the Kansas Newman College Library; and Sandy Echt, Mary Charlotte Ferris, Janna Ferguson, Sally Brady, Brenda Barnes, and Ruth Ross of Mary Couts Burnett Library at Texas Christian University.

I would especially like to thank my wife, Karen Capell, and my daughter, Meghan, for their patience, understanding, and assistance throughout the course of this project.

1. Introduction

Most of the Indians whose names are still remembered were warriors—Tecumseh, Black Hawk, Sitting Bull, Crazy Horse, Geronimo—men who led their people in a desperate defense of their lands and their way of life.[1] As celebrated figures in American frontier lore, their adventures have filled the pages of many books. "They were big men," writes Alvin M. Josephy, "as much a part of our heritage as any of our other heroes, and they belong to all Americans now, not just to the Indians." They were, Josephy rightly asserts, the Indian equivalents of Nathan Hale, George Washington, and Benjamin Franklin. But Josephy admits that these were only the most renowned Indian heroes, the few who penetrated the white man's consciousness. "Some of the Indians' greatest patriots died unsung by white men," he notes, "and because their peoples were also obliterated, or almost so, their names are forgotten."[2]

Kenekuk, of the Vermillion Band of Kickapoos and Potawatomis who were living along the Wabash and Vermillion rivers in Indiana and Illinois, was one of those unsung patriots.[3] From the 1820s to 1852, this "Kickapoo Prophet" displayed exceptional leadership in helping his followers to adjust to white society and retain their lands, without resorting to warfare or losing their identity as Indians. Because he represented only a small band of peaceful

Indians, instead of a large force of warriors such as the Brulé Sioux, the Comanches, or the Apaches, Kenekuk's achievements have been largely overlooked. Yet his leadership, which was based on peace and love, was no less astute and courageous than that of the bravest war chief, and his teachings continued to guide his people long after his death. In his policies, as well as in his influence, he was unique among American Indians.

Kenekuk first attracted attention during the great religious revival of the 1820s and 1830s, when white visitors, such as the famous artist George Catlin, observed that the prophet's fiery sermons often aroused his listeners to a fever pitch. At prayer meetings similar to those held by Charles Grandison Finney, one of the nineteenth century's most renowned evangelists, Kenekuk taught that every human heart was "the fountain from which good or evil thoughts flow," and he admonished his followers to respect the Great Spirit's commands: "You are all sinners; you cannot be too much on your guard, lest you tread out of the right way into the broad road." He warned those who flouted God's laws that they would be banished to the pits of hell, pits "filled with fire for the punishment of all wicked . . . men; all professed drunkards, tattlers, liars, and meddling bodies are in the broad way; they never can be received into good places, their deeds are dark, they never see light."[4] Like Finney's, Kenekuk's gospel combined faith and good works; miracles were not needed for salvation. There was also little room for Calvinistic predestination in Kenekuk's plan: all who rejected evil and led religious lives would be saved.

The prophet's zeal and energy went far beyond saving souls, for he was also an effective leader who understood the ways both of whites and of his own people. During the 1820s Kenekuk founded a pragmatic, rational, and enduring religion that helped to ensure a relatively secure future for his Kickapoo and Potawatomi adherents in a land dominated by predatory whites. Unlike Tenskwatawa—the Shawnee Prophet—and his brother Tecumseh, whose warlike actions proved disastrous for their people, the Kickapoo leader always stressed peace and outward cooperation with whites. Frontier settlers from Indiana to Kansas therefore came to accept his people as neighbors, instead of branding them as enemies. Whites had to admit, moreover, that the prophet's basic values were similar to their own; Kenekuk's followers obeyed similar systems of social control and law, adopted modern agricultural methods, understood and lived by Euro-American economic practices, and followed a religion that resembled Christianity.

The prophet's emergence as a chief helped reinforce and give focus to a movement that began when he was still a child.[5] Some time during the 1790s, after the Indians of the Ohio Valley had suffered a series of defeats at the hands of American soldiers, many Vermillion Kickapoos and their allies sought an accommodation with whites that would allow those Indians to maintain a separate cultural identity. They consciously began to build a social structure that would enable them to survive as Indians under changing conditions that were beyond their control.

By the time Kenekuk became their religious and secular leader in the 1820s, the Indians had nearly completed a full regeneration of their traditional way of life. The prophet's commanding presence helped to reinforce an ongoing effort to survive and prosper by remolding Indian customs to conform to the realities of their changing environment. His message of peace (and frequently of passive resistance to governmental authority) proved effective, for his people fared better than most Indians. Before his death in 1852, Kenekuk had prepared his people for the challenge of maintaining a separate and unique Indian way of life within a dominant American culture.

The prophet's religion strengthened the innovative trend of Vermillion Kickapoo and Potawatomi culture and provided an effective vehicle for carrying the Indians into the modern world. Under Kenekuk's guidance, his people came to realize that walking the fine line between Indian and white society was their best chance for survival. For them, complete assimilation was not the answer; their cultural traditions were too important to be forgotten completely. While other bands disintegrated because they either resisted cultural innovations or assimilated under stress, the Vermillion people prospered. Kenekuk showed them how to retain important cultural practices while making certain modifications when necessary. He realized that even if the Indians wanted to enter the American mainstream, white racism precluded that possibility.

This study is about Kenekuk and his efforts to bring about the acculturation of his people to American society. He realized that if his followers outwardly adapted to American culture, they could win the grudging respect of whites, who would then accept them as members of the overall community. But while Kenekuk's people ultimately accepted acculturation, they never chose to assimilate: although they lived *like* whites, they did not live *as* whites. Although this distinction is sometimes difficult for outsiders to recognize, it exists even today. The Indians themselves realize that they are culturally different from other Americans, and they cherish that difference.

By definition, the process of acculturation differs from assimilation. The latter involves the total absorption of an immigrant or minority group into the cultural and traditional mainstream of a dominant population. One who has assimilated has lost or rejected all elements of his or her former cultural heritage. Governmental officials, federal troops, missionaries, schoolteachers, and others endeavored to coerce Indians and other minority groups to assimilate. The government's civilization and reservation policies, backed by military force, were attempts to make Indians forget or discard all vestiges of their traditional cultures. Against the wishes of parents, officials took Indian children and isolated them in boarding schools, away from their traditional cultures, languages, religions, dress, and everything else that the whites deemed uncivilized. But even the most drastic measures failed to achieve the ends that federal officials had hoped to accomplish. Many Indians simply refused to assimilate.

Indians were more willing to accept acculturation—the process of intercultural borrowing between two or more diverse peoples that results in a new and blended culture. This can be a one-sided process, as it was with the Vermillion Kickapoos and white Americans: obviously, the Kickapoos and their allies have adopted far more white cultural traits than vice versa. Although many minority ethnic groups have been thoroughly assimilated into the dominant American culture, Kenekuk's Kickapoos and Potawatomis never considered assimilation desirable. Acculturation, to the prophet's followers, was simply a defense mechanism, a means to survive as a people by making minor concessions.

As the historian Henry Warner Bowden points out, the advocates of assimilation for Indians failed to notice that the principal obstacle to their plans "was rooted in Indian spirituality, a wellspring of inner strength not easily affected by superficial changes. As long as independent religious vitality survived, it filled Indians with a sense of their own identity and cultural importance, with a power that defied alien control." Unified by Kenekuk's teachings, the Vermillion Kickapoos and Potawatomis achieved their goal of retaining a separate identity—they remained American Indians—while being accepted as part of the white community.

Today, those descendants of Kenekuk and his followers who live on the Kansas reservation and elsewhere still recognize that they are different from other Americans— they take pride in a difference that is by no means a badge of shame. They speak English and dress like their white neighbors, attend formal schools and earn college degrees, own farms or work in factories, serve the United States in peace and in war, and even attend Catholic and Protestant churches; but they proudly preserve their Indian heritage. They owe their survival as a people, in large part, to Kenekuk and his intrepid followers, who held fast to their lands and way of life.

2. The Vermillion Band Kickapoos

From the time when Europeans first invaded their lands, American Indians have had to adapt and adjust to constantly changing social circumstances. The culturally diverse tribes held their own against the intruders at first, but as the years went by, increasing numbers of the technologically advanced Europeans arrived and the number of Indians declined. By the early nineteenth century, Euro-Americans were dominant from the Atlantic seaboard to the Mississippi River. After the War of 1812, land-hungry frontiersmen and politicians steadily pressured the hapless eastern Indians into surrendering their lands and moving west of the Mississippi. Settlers, businessmen, missionaries, and governmental officials agreed that for the United States to prosper, the Indians must go. White Americans thought that it was God's will that the Indians should move: Manifest Destiny must never be held in check! At the same time they rationalized that moving was in the best interest of the Indians.

The Vermillion Kickapoos, who lived along the Indiana-Illinois border, were among those who faced intense pressure to give up their lands. The Kickapoos were one of the many Algonquin tribes that lived in the Old Northwest region of North America. Algonquins, such as Kickapoos, Delawares, Potawatomis, Miamis, Shawnees, and Sacs and Foxes, shared common cultural and religious traits as well as similar

The Wabash-Vermillion region.

languages. During the spring and summer, these hunters, gatherers, and horticulturists lived in villages, planted crops, and carried out tribal activities. During the rest of the year, the bands split into smaller units to hunt deer and other game—sometimes ranging hundreds of miles from their semipermanent villages.

By the late eighteenth century the Kickapoos and other Algonquin tribes were reacting in various ways to the influx of whites into their territories. Some bands endeavored to appease the invaders by abandoning their traditional ways, adopting white manners and customs, and trying to blend into mainstream American life. When that failed, they eventually surrendered their homes and reluctantly moved beyond the Mississippi. Other bands resorted to violence to drive the whites from their lands. The Great Spirit, they believed, would come to their aid and help to restore them to their former power. The Shawnee prophet Tenskwatawa, his brother Tecumseh, and Black Hawk, of the Sacs and Foxes, led futile uprisings against the powerful Americans. Such resistance may have endeared these warriors to modern scholars and history buffs, but the results proved disastrous for their followers.

Beginning sometime around 1795, various bands of Vermillion Kickapoos adopted a different strategy in dealing with the problems they were facing. These Indians sought to accommodate themselves to the white society while at the same time maintaining a separate cultural identity. They began a conscious effort to revitalize their culture and to build a social structure that would better satisfy their needs in a changing world![1]

To make themselves more acceptable to their white neighbors, these Kickapoos began to assume the trappings of American society. At the same time, they restructured certain important aspects of their traditional culture. They discarded practices that were no longer appropriate to their changed environment, such as warfare and a reliance on hunting; and they heeded the government's advice to settle down, build homes, and farm the land. Their effort was a practical way of coping with a difficult situation; it was a peaceful quest to keep their lands. Their new syncretic society combined, modified, altered, and discarded certain aspects of both the Kickapoo and the Euro-American ways. This cultural blend provided the Indians with a strong defense against white assaults on their tribal integrity as well as their lands.[2]

Like other Algonquins, the Vermillion Kickapoos had experienced years of cultural interaction with white society. By the mid-1700s, the introduction of European trade goods had greatly altered their traditional social and economic structures, and disease had decimated their populations. Christian missionaries, moreover, had attempted to make over Kickapoo habits and customs in accordance with the missionaries' own notions of civilized behavior. But unlike many of the other tribes that willingly made some accommodation with the intruders, the Kickapoos traditionally showed open hostility to whites who meddled in their affairs. Traders and missionaries were especially cautious in dealing with the Kickapoos, who frequently resorted to violence to expel intruders from their territory. While willing to modify their ways, the Kickapoos were determined to be the final arbiters of the form that those modifications would take.

Described by modern scholars as the most culturally conservative of North American Indians, Kickapoos often gathered in groups around influential leaders. Bands numbered between fifty and four hundred individuals, while the population of the entire tribe during the nineteenth century has been estimated at fifteen hundred. Usually preferring to live as far as possible from white settlements, the Kickapoos were particularly hostile to Anglo-Americans, and on many occasions the various bands chose to move instead of risking a confrontation with invading white settlers.[3] By the late eighteenth century, however, a few Kickapoo bands had begun to see the need to make some accommodation. These Indians decided to adapt to changing conditions in their country, rather than moving to a place far distant from white interference.

Within the tribe, two major groups emerged that responded in markedly different ways to white incursions. Since the early 1700s, the Vermillion people had lived in the Wabash country along both sides of the present Indiana-Illinois border; other Kickapoo bands had moved from their native Wisconsin and settled in the prairies of central and western Illinois. Because of the physical separation, the cultures of the Vermillion bands and the Prairie Kickapoos evolved somewhat differently. The Prairie bands were, by tradition, hostile to whites and preferred to live as far as possible from their settlements. Many times during the eighteenth and nineteenth centuries they chose to move rather than deal with wave after wave of American settlers. In contrast, by 1795 many Vermillion Indians had developed a binding love for their lands and refused to move. So strong did this attachment to the land grow that one chief directed that he be buried on the banks of the Wabash River when he died; if his followers sold their lands, he told them, they would also be selling "his body, and their flesh."[4]

Stung by defeats during the Revolutionary War and by various later conflicts with the Americans, the Wabash-Vermillion bands realized that in order to survive they had to live peacefully, so they began a movement to revitalize their way of life. For years after 1795 they remained in "quiet possession of the country," avoiding conflict with incoming settlers as much as possible.[5] As a continuous stream of Americans poured into the Ohio Valley and settlements sprang up in Indiana and Illinois, however, encroachments on these Indians' lands increased. Whites beseeched local politicians and federal officials to coerce even peaceful Indians, such as the Vermillion people, to abandon their homes. Negotiations with the tribes eventually began, and by the end of the first decade of the nineteenth century, the Kickapoos and others had ceded large tracts of land. Under increasingly difficult circumstances, retaining the rest of their holdings became the foremost concern of the tribes of the Old Northwest.

Like many other Indians in the Ohio Valley, the Shawnee Prophet and his brother Tecumseh were angered by white encroachments on their territory. They were especially irate after the Treaty of Fort Wayne of September 30, 1809. In that agreement, Indiana's Governor William Henry Harrison persuaded various Miami, Potawatomi, and Delaware "chiefs" to part with three million acres of Indian lands in exchange for increased governmental annuities and trade goods.

Harrison mistakenly believed that the power that the Shawnee brothers possessed to rally Indians against such spurious land cessions had diminished. But the governor had greatly underestimated the Shawnee Prophet and Tecumseh. What set them apart from other Indians was the scope and power of their plans for dealing with the invasion of their lands. Preaching the need for an intertribal defense against the white Americans, the brothers urged all tribes to join together to protect their mutual interests. If the Indians would reject white customs and return to their traditional ways, the brothers preached, the Great Spirit would aid them in their quest. As spiritual leader of the Indians, the Shawnee Prophet urged his followers to remain strong by abstaining from alcohol, wearing Indian clothing, practicing traditional ceremonies, and worshiping the Great Spirit. His message of intertribal unity met receptive ears. When Tecumseh, an astute military strategist, toured Indian country seeking cooperation, Shawnees, Winnebagos, Potawatomis, Sacs, Foxes, Kickapoos, and other bands joined the crusade. By 1810 hundreds of warriors had united with the brothers, causing alarm among white settlements, and war seemed to be inevitable.[6]

The conflict came in November 1811, when Governor Harrison's troops attacked Prophetstown on the Tippecanoe River. Because Harrison's troops had stormed through their villages on their way to attack the Shawnees, many Kickapoos joined with Tecumseh and the Shawnee Prophet in the subsequent War of 1812. But while many bands of Shawnee, Potawatomi, Kickapoo, and other Indians rallied to the intertribal cause, Vermillion Kickapoo leaders took steps to keep their followers peaceful. One Kickapoo chief sought to avert conflict by warning Harrison about Tecumseh's warlike intentions. After that effort had failed, another Vermillion leader traveled to Vincennes in December 1811 to seek peace. Although he, too, was unsuccessful, many Kickapoos still tried to remain neutral, and in the following spring one hundred and fifty Vermillion Indians visited Vincennes in order to express friendship toward the Americans.

The war dragged on, however, and the Indians paid a heavy price. In October 1812, for example, three hundred militia volunteers ambushed a Prairie Kickapoo village near the Sangamon River in central Illinois. The troops destroyed four thousand bushels of corn, as well as a large quantity of meat, beans, pumpkins, and animal skins. As the frightened Indians fled into a nearby swamp, the attackers burnt the village to the ground.[7]

Fortunately for the Indians, the hostilities had waned by December 1814, when a Vermillion chief and his followers appeared at Fort Harrison, near present-day Terre Haute, to express their continued "amity and good will" toward the Americans. Tired of war, the Kickapoos were determined to make a lasting peace, and they left on friendly terms, even though a white man had murdered a Kickapoo woman at the fort.[8] For the next several months these Indians struggled to maintain their territorial boundaries, which the war had rendered unclear. Retaining their lands had become the foremost concern of the Vermillion Kickapoos.

Protecting their holdings became increasingly difficult as more whites invaded the Old Northwest after the War of 1812. Conflicts between such culturally different peoples who were competing for the same land were inevitable. Both Indians and whites used roughly the same amount of land for farming, but settlers relied on domesticated animals for meat, whereas most Kickapoos and other Indians depended on hunting. Because hunters required a large territory to satisfy their needs, whites insisted that their own methods of land use were superior. They farmed intensively and "improved" the soil, whereas the "lazy" Indian hunters merely "roamed" over the land. To whites who were influenced by the Protestant work ethic, hunting was a sport, not honest labor. They justified Indian removal on the grounds that the tribes had failed to use the land as God had intended. Each white farmer, moreover, held legal title to his own land. Policy makers were convinced that only when the tribesmen would accept deeds to individual farms could they be considered truly civilized. Until then, the Indians constituted an impediment to "progress" and to the proper utilization of land.

Time and again the vastly different methods of using available lands brought forth hard feelings. During the 1810s, for example, citizens demanded that the federal government use force to prevent the loss of "fertile tracts of earth to perpetual sterility as the hunting ground" for Indians. Most citizens were in agreement with Governor Harrison, when he demanded to know if "one of the finest portions of the globe [Indiana] is to remain in the state of nature, the haunt of a few wretched savages."[9]

After the War of 1812, American political leaders acted to ensure that this would not happen. The Louisiana Purchase of 1803 had more than doubled the territory of the United States, and the vast lands beyond the Mississippi seemed an ideal place to move the Indians who were still living in the East. Frustrated that most tribes resisted assimilation into American society, Presidents Jefferson, Madison, and Monroe had each reasoned that removal to the West was in the best interests of the Indians as well as the whites. Removal would open eastern lands to industrious white farmers and would give the Indians more time to learn the ways of civilization without interference from politicians and settlers.

During 1815 and 1816, federal officials, hoping to put their removal plans into motion, sought peace agreements with Potawatomis, Sacs and Foxes, Kickapoos, and other former belligerents. Once the prospects for permanent peace were enhanced, Indian agents in Indiana and Illinois could begin the delicate land-cession negotiations with the tribes. Although the government hoped to move the tribes beyond the Mississippi within a few years, removal efforts proceeded slowly. The Kickapoos and other Indians were still a powerful factor in sparsely settled Illinois, and agents could ill afford to antagonize them. Unable to use force, the Indian agents tried to strike the best bargains possible by relying on friendly persuasion and deception in their dealings with the tribes.[10]

Illinois Territory's Governor Ninian Edwards recommended that a judicious approach be taken, especially with the Prairie Kickapoos, with whom he had concluded a peace agreement in September 1815. He said later that these Indians were "much the bravest and most warlike of all neighboring savages." Better to keep them friendly, Edwards advised, because they could act as "a barrier against the inroads of all plunderers." With this in mind, federal officials, who could barely distinguish between the many different tribes, much less the various bands, began peace negotiations with the Vermillion Kickapoos early in the following year.[11]

In late May 1816, nearly five hundred Vermillion Kickapoos and Weas gathered at Fort Harrison to conclude a treaty. The Indians had reason to be especially joyous, for they would finally receive the long-overdue annuities promised in earlier treaties; they were also gratified that the new agreement included no further land cessions. On May 26 the Indians held a dance to celebrate the occasion. One white visitor reported that throughout the night, Indians as old as seventy and as young as four danced around a campfire to the sounds of drums and singing.[12]

On June 4, pledging to maintain the territorial boundaries that had been established before the war, the Kickapoo chiefs and headmen signed the treaty.[13] Prominent among the signers, after the leading chief Little Duck, was Kenekuk—the "Drunkard's Son." Because his father was an alcoholic, Kenekuk knew well the danger of intemperance, which was unfortunately dramatized after the treaty ceremonies. An observer noted that when "whiskey was liberally dealt out," a "frenzy of intoxication" ensued, and one Indian murdered another. To prevent further trouble, fellow tribesmen acted quickly to put the offender to death.[14] Because whites believed that such behavior was typical of "red savages," men such as Kenekuk realized that the Indians must change their ways if they were to survive peacefully among the whites.

Because officials in Indiana and Illinois knew that they had to extend a "liberal" policy toward Indians "for two or three years at least,"[15] they also wanted the Indians to change their ways. Indiana's Governor Thomas Posey believed that white settlement of his state would proceed more rapidly if the Indians could somehow be absorbed into the mainstream of American society. On November 22, 1816, Posey addressed 760 Weas, Potawatomis, and Vermillion Kickapoos who were assembled at Fort Harrison. In a speech that outwardly was religious in tone, the governor commanded the Indians to "set about immediately to alter your mode of life." His talk amounted to a wholesale denunciation of traditional Indian ways. Ignoring the fact that most of them were already farmers, he advised them to follow the example of the successful Cherokees and other southern tribesmen who had abandoned hunting to till the soil.

Posey stressed the necessity of adopting Christian values and Euro-American forms of social organization. Telling the assembled Indians that their old ways were sinful, he preached that they should "love the Great Spirit and keep his laws," for an angry God would punish wrongdoers "in this world or in the world where our spirits go." In fine paternalistic fashion, Posey informed his Indian "children" that they would serve God and achieve success only by building permanent villages, raising crops and livestock, learning the "useful arts," and providing their offspring with a formal education. The Indians, most of whom were undoubtedly offended by the governor's sanctimonious attitude, listened more attentively when he promised financial assistance to all who accepted his proposals. Those assembled, including the Vermillion Kickapoo leader Little Duck, would not refuse governmental help in improving their living conditions and in securing permanent title to their lands.[16]

The Vermillion Kickapoos realized that their hold on the lands was becoming increasingly tenuous. Whites, who were grasping at any excuse to take control of Indian holdings, asserted that some tribes that had sided with Great Britain during the War 1812 should be banished. Even those who had been neutral or loyal to the United States would have to go. Settlers and politicians in the Old Northwest and the southern states beseeched the federal government to force the Indians, regardless of their allegiance during the war, to make way for the axe and the plow of "civilization." Federal officials sympathized and began to seek ways in which to solve the Indian "problem" to the satisfaction of the frontiersmen. Citizens had political clout and were a force to be reckoned with, so the needs of Indians were of secondary importance.

Settlers who were flooding into Illinois Territory in 1817 clamored for control of the fertile Indian lands. One traveler called Illinois the finest location in North America: "The timber, the herbage, [and] the animals themselves that feed upon it are evidence of this." So marvelous were its "woods and prairies, gently rising hills and widely extended vallies, that one may choose a paradise for a residence in almost any part of it."[17] Federal officials also recognized the value of the territory, and on February 28, 1817, the acting secretary of war, George Graham, authorized Governor Edwards to investigate whether the Indians of central and western Illinois would be willing to sell their lands.[18]

The Prairie Kickapoos were among the principal tribes affected by Graham's order, because they controlled lands from the Sangamon valley west to the Illinois River. Anxious to open the area to white settlement, Governor Edwards asserted that the federal government was authorized to remove the Kickapoos from the land, for they had "no right whatever to it, except mere occupancy." Although the band had lived there since the 1730s and their legal right to the land was sound, Edwards alleged that they had been in the area for only a short time. He admitted that they had hunted in central Illinois for years, but he maintained that the tribe's real home lay to the east, along the Wabash and its tributaries.[19]

Meanwhile, half-hearted governmental efforts to "civilize" and assimilate the eastern tribes fell afoul of land-hungry settlers. Frontiersmen and local politicians argued that absorbing the Indians into "civilized society without unpleasant collisions [was] about as probable as to expect a union between fire and water for mutual existence." Washington bureaucrats took heed, and the old Jeffersonian Enlightenment ideas that allowed for the gradual assimilation of Indians faded quickly from the minds of most officials. While the explorer William Clark and a few others still believed that the Indians were capable of advancing to a level of civilization comparable to that of whites, the frontiersmen were not willing to wait for that to occur. Most frontiersmen thought of Indians as savages who were not capable of advancement, and politicians were quick to agree. Officials increasingly argued that protecting the interests of westward-moving settlers would better serve the nation than would upholding the rights of Indians.[20]

Economy-minded officials at the Indian Department in Washington concluded that governmental expenditures were far too high for tribesmen who were about to be moved west;

therefore they ordered stringent reductions. Annuity payments, which were guaranteed to the tribes under previous treaties, were withheld, and promised farm implements, food, and clothing arrived either late or not at all. Only when governmental indifference and inefficiency began to hinder removal efforts did the Indian agents urge officials in Washington to be less frugal. The special treaty commissioner Auguste Chouteau, a St. Louis businessman, stated in July 1818 that unless the tribes received their annuity payments promptly, all land-cession negotiations were doomed to failure.[21]

Pressure from Illinois whites exacerbated the tensions surrounding removal. By 1819, citizens of the new state were pressing harder for a rapid settlement of the Indian question. Most believed that if their state was to attract more settlers, they would have to change the eastern perception that they were "venturesome daredevils" living among "savage red men."[22] In January 1819 the *Illinois Intelligencer* (Kaskaskia) reported on the long-tried governmental plan "to draw the attention of these wild men of the chase to the culture of the earth; and so far as practicable, to incorporate them with the American citizens." But even as the paper's editors were wondering just how long it would take the Indians to advance "from the savage to the civilized state,"[23] efforts to remove the tribes from the Old Northwest began to bear fruit.

In the summer of 1819, federal commissioners managed to persuade the Prairie Kickapoos to surrender all of their claims to Illinois lands. That July, leaders of the Prairie bands arrived at Edwardsville, Illinois, to consider a move to central Missouri. To white townspeople, the Kickapoos were a "most remarkable curiosity." One astonished onlooker noted that "their color is reddish brown; their face irregular, often horribly colored with bright red paint; their hair is cut to a tuft upon the crown of the head and painted various colors." They wore scant clothing, but they hung silver rings about their necks and arms and carried shields.[24] On July 30 the Indians met with commissioners Chouteau and Benjamin Stephenson, and in exchange for yearly annuities and promises of governmental assistance on new lands near the Osage River in Missouri, the chiefs relinquished approximately fourteen million acres of prime Illinois land.[25]

After successfully negotiating the treaty with the Prairie Kickapoos, officials began to negotiate with the Vermillion bands in the hope of achieving a similar coup. On August 10, Indian Agent Benjamin Parke informed Secretary of War John C. Calhoun that an agreement appeared imminent. Indeed, just two days later Agent William Prince reported that "the Vermillion Kickapoos [had] determined to cede to the United States their country west of the Wabash River without reserve." Prince wrote that he needed only a few days to prepare for the treaty council, because "an understanding" had already been reached with these Indians—that understanding included a promise to pay a total of $3,000 to "chiefs" who were willing to sign the treaty.

Prince had shrewdly avoided discussions with such Vermillion leaders as Little Duck, who represented the great majority of Indians and strongly disagreed with selling their homes and lands. Typically, agents such as Prince dealt with those who were willing to accept bribes and who would sign anything in exchange for money, trade goods, or whiskey. Unfortunately, such devious methods were almost always successful. Ignorant of the white man's law and unable to take legal recourse, incorruptible Indians usually lacked the means to combat such schemes. Prince was so confident that he would win an "advantageous" agreement from the Vermillion bands that he asked the secretary of war for only enough provisions to carry out short-term negotiations.[26]

At Fort Harrison on August 30, 1819, the Vermillion "chiefs" agreed to surrender their Indiana-Illinois homeland. Because the Vermillion people had shown signs of accommodation to American society and because they were generally on friendly terms with their white neighbors, the treaty failed to specify immediate removal to the West. Eventually, however, federal officials hoped to rid the East of all Indians, regardless of circumstances. Secretary of War Calhoun made the government's intentions and rationalizations clear that September. It was desirable, he stated, to remove the Kickapoos and other Indians beyond the Mississippi, "where a more extensive scope is afforded for the indulgence of their barbarous propensities and habits."[27]

Calhoun and other bureaucrats wanted the Indians to make room for the supposedly more industrious white farmers, and these officials were confident that their plans would be implemented with relative speed. The removal process, however, met with many obstacles; it would take more than thirty years to complete. Most Vermillion Kickapoos had no intention of ever abandoning their sacred homelands, and prying them from their tenacious hold proved far more difficult than was anticipated.

During the years after the land-cession treaties, several Prairie and Vermillion Kickapoos moved to Missouri, but most of them clung to their lands and refused to leave. Mecina, or Elk Horn, a leader of one of the Prairie bands living along the Sangamon River, argued that the Treaty of Edwardsville was not binding on him because he had never signed it. Mecina demanded to know what right the government had "to purchase lands from the Red Skins, because it was very injurious to the Indians to sell, swap, or buy

Mecina, or Elk Horn. The Prairie Kickapoo leader and his followers became adherents of the prophet's religion. Courtesy of the Thomas Gilcrease Institute of American History and Art.

lands." He threatened to burn down any houses that whites might build in the territory.[28]

Along the Wabash River and its tributaries, several Vermillion bands also remained. During the questionable negotiations that preceded the signing of the treaty at Fort

Harrison, a new leader had risen among them. This charismatic man believed that selling land violated the Great Spirit's commands, and he strenuously resisted all attempts to evict his followers. Like Mecina, this Indian had not signed any treaty surrendering Kickapoo lands.[29] During the 1820s and afterwards, employing the tactics of white society to the Indians' advantage, he proved to be a thorn in the side of governmental officials, missionaries, and other whites who attempted to meddle in Kickapoo affairs. Not surprisingly, he followed the prescription for success that Indiana's Governor Posey had laid down in 1816—but with a new and different emphasis. He was Kenekuk, the Kickapoo Prophet.

3. Instructed by the Great Spirit

Although Little Duck and Kenekuk had both signed the 1816 treaty by which they and the Vermillion Kickapoos had agreed to "acknowledge themselves in peace and friendship with the United States," neither was consulted about the 1819 cession treaty. Federal officials realized that the two men would have absolutely refused to sell tribal lands and therefore avoided dealing with them. Both had been born in the Indiana-Illinois region and had grown up near the Wabash and its tributaries. Both had hunted deer along the wooded streams near their homes and buffalo in the immense prairies far to the west. They had played lacrosse and other traditional games, defended their families against Indian and white enemies, married and raised children, buried relatives and friends, and participated in the numerous ceremonies of the Kickapoo bands and clans. They loved their Wabash homeland, and they knew that the Great Spirit would be angry if they voluntarily abandoned it.

By the early 1820s, however, the aged Little Duck was too feeble to continue his long struggle in defense of the Vermillion people. He had led them courageously for many years, advising them to remain peaceful and to seek an accommodation with white settlers in order to retain their Wabash lands. He wisely turned the reins of leadership over to Kenekuk, who could give a strong voice and charismatic direction to the tribal revitalization movement that had been under way since the 1790s. Little Duck was undoubtedly confident that Kenekuk was now ready to guide his people through the trying years ahead.[2]

Little is known of Kenekuk's life before he emerged as an influential spokesman for the Vermillion bands during the 1820s. The tribe had kept relatively few written or official records before that time, but Kickapoo oral tradition reveals some clues as to his early years. He was born about 1790 or 1791,[3] probably near the banks of the Wabash River some distance from modern Lafayette, Indiana. As a young man, according to tribal accounts, he was a drunken beggar of violent behavior:

> Kenekuk was a bad young man, a drunkard. Once while in a drunken rage he killed his own uncle. For this reason he was banished from the tribe. He therefore went to live on the outskirts of the white frontier settlements, making a living doing odd jobs.
>
> A white man, a "priest," felt pity for the young outcast and took him as a helper around the house. One day the priest happened to come upon Kenekuk while the latter was looking through some religious books in the priest's library. The priest asked Kenekuk what he was doing, and Kenekuk replied that he wished to know what was in these books. The priest replied that the books contained the teachings of the white man's religion, and that the whites put great store in them. Impressed, Kenekuk asked if he might learn the teachings. The priest consented and the instruction began.
>
> Later, noting his pupil's progress, the priest told Kenekuk that if he brought these good teachings back to his own people he would be forgiven by them for the murder of his uncle, as this would atone for his sin.
>
> Kenekuk applied himself to his studies, and, after he had

learned the fundamentals of the white man's religion from the priest, he brought his own version of what he had learned back to the Kickapoos. As the priest had predicted, Kenekuk was forgiven. Not only was he allowed to return to his tribe and marry, but he also became a leader among them.[4]

Kenekuk was in his mid-twenties when he returned to a people weary of defending themselves and their homes in the War of 1812.[5] By the end of that conflict, even many of those Vermillion Kickapoos who had fought alongside Tecumseh and the Shawnee Prophet were ready to listen to the words of peace and coexistence that Kenekuk had brought with him. Whites who met the Kickapoo Prophet in later years assumed that his preachings of peace and salvation were based solely on Christianity, learned from a priest or a kindly minister. It was Kenekuk's own interpretation of the Scriptures, however, that he preached to the Kickapoos and other Indians in the Indiana-Illinois region. In fact, his gospel departed significantly from conventional Christianity; it contained an implicit cultural nationalism that merged with, rather than superseded, traditional Indian beliefs.

Shortly after his return, sometime around 1815, the Kickapoo Prophet began telling his people that they had wandered far from God's teachings. For this reason the Great Spirit had abandoned them, and they had been defeated and dispersed in wars and had lost valuable lands. But according to Kenekuk, God felt lonely and sorrowful without His beloved Kickapoos, and He now had returned to earth to redeem them. God had chosen to reveal Himself through Kenekuk—the Indian Moses—to whom He had left His sacred black coat. By wearing this black coat—God's holy garment—Kenekuk proved to all that he alone had been ordained to guide his people down the true path. The Indians therefore must no longer pay heed to the alien notions of Protestant ministers or Catholic priests: they should ignore white men dressed in similar black clothing.

The Great Spirit had also given Kenekuk a piece of His heart, which would instruct the Indians in the ways of peace and love. "God took out . . . His own heart," the Kickapoo Prophet explained, "and sent [it] to teach the red man the way in which he should go." The Great Spirit's "heart [is] filled with good knowledge," and through Kenekuk it "speaks" to the Indians: "This [heart] is from your Father, my children, worship Me."[6]

The Great Spirit's message, delivered through the Kickapoo Prophet, reached the receptive ears of many. Whites were appalled that some Indians actually believed that Kenekuk was the son of God, but they missed the point; it mattered little to the Indians whether Kenekuk was a man or a deity. He was one of them—a fellow tribesman, not a missionary, government official, trader, or settler—a man who was seeking to help them, not to steal their lands or force them to abandon their traditions. The Indians accepted him because he spoke in terms that they understood. Preferring their traditional religious practices, the Kickapoos consistently rejected the overtures of Catholic and Protestant missionaries. Although Kenekuk's new religion was by no means traditional, it suited the needs of the Vermillion people. They could adopt useful aspects of Christianity, but they did not have to reject the ancient sacred customs, which white ministers insisted that they abandon.

Instead, Kenekuk's syncretic religion allowed them to combine the old ways with the new. As the English traveler Charles Augustus Murray observed, this "miniature Mahomet" had grafted his knowledge of Christianity "upon his Indian prejudices and superstitions."[7] Yet the basic Christian structure of the new religion was clearly evident; to outsiders the ceremonies seemed to be primitive Roman Catholic rituals. "Their religion and worship in all their parts," wrote the Presbyterian missionary William D. Smith, "seem to bear a striking resemblance to that of the Roman Catholics, and whatever notions of Christianity they may have, they are . . . decidedly of that character." The Baptist preacher Isaac McCoy also recognized the similarities between Kenekuk's religion and Catholicism: "The formula of the Prophet had evidently not been framed from ideas purely Indian, and they more nearly resembled those of the Catholics than any other sect." The Jesuit priest Benedict Roux also noted the similarities. "It is enough to say to you that they are truly Catholic in desire," he told his superiors, "and such Catholics in desire that their life gives you a perfect image of that of Christians of the primitive church."[8]

On the surface, such assessments were accurate, for Kenekuk's religion had adopted many aspects of Catholicism. In Wisconsin over a century earlier, Jesuit priests had exposed the Kickapoos and other tribes to the prayers and rituals of the Roman Catholic faith. After settling in the area between the Wabash and Vermillion rivers in the eighteenth century, the Kickapoos had lost contact with the priests but had continued to practice some of the Catholic rites. Under Kenekuk these observances were reinforced and intensified.

Indeed, the prophet's followers worshiped Jesus, the Virgin, and the saints; and they believed in heaven, hell, and purgatory. They also faithfully attended formal services on Sundays and holy days. On a typical Sunday, "criers" ran through the villages, calling believers together for services. As the people arrived, the men moved to one side, the women to the other, the children gathered in between, and everyone stood before a roaring fire in the center of the grounds. After eating a feast prepared by Kenekuk's most devout adherents, the congregation entered the "church" and sat while the prophet held forth, sometimes for an hour or longer, followed by one or more additional speakers. When they had finished, the celebrants all shook hands and returned to their lodges. One white witness recalled that "no congregation, even in the days of the Puritan fathers, was more decorous" than these Indians.[9]

While looking on during one Kickapoo ceremony that was held under a large, open reed-thatched structure, Charles Murray also noted that the "meeting was conducted with the greatest decorum." The Indian men removed their hats before entering the hut, just as Catholics did at Mass. After a sermon by one of Kenekuk's assistants, the ardent congregation sang a hymn. "It was [of] a low, melancholy, and not unmusical air," wrote Murray, "and was rendered wild and peculiar by the closing of each verse in the minor key." Spellbound by the fascinating religious rite, the white visitor allowed himself to "entertain hopes, though but faint ones, that this twilight may be the forerunner of the sunrise of the Gospel" among these people.[10]

Men such as Murray found encouragement in the fact that like a Protestant evangelist, the Kickapoo Prophet spoke out against sin and employed the threat of hell in his sermons. "The Great Father gave you a good book filled with commands," Kenekuk reminded his listeners: "If you follow the commands, you will go into a good place and be happy forever; but if you do not keep them, you will go into a place prepared for the wicked and suffer endless days and nights of grief." He was convinced that alcoholism threatened the very existence of his people, and he railed against that evil. Those "with bloated faces and swelled eyes occasioned by drunkenness," he warned, must either find the good road or face eternal damnation. The Son of the Great Spirit "is to come once more, when the wicked will not be noticed by Him—a great many hundreds will be lost; then we will see who has obeyed His book and kept His commands." Kenekuk predicted that God would soon destroy the evil world: "No supplication will then avail—you will have no opportunity to kneel to Him—the time is past, He will not allow it; your friends cannot intercede—fear will overwhelm you—you will wish to make new resolutions to obey Him, but you cannot, you will go to the burning pits."[11]

Kenekuk's adherents could avoid hell fire and brimstone only by renouncing their sins at public confessions on Fridays. But unlike Catholics who earned absolution from a priest by reciting silent prayers, the Indian penitents demanded physical evidence that God had cleansed their souls; therefore, after admitting their wrongful acts, they eagerly submitted to the whip. Illinois settler Patrick Hopkins witnessed one ceremony at which, after a sermon by the prophet and several hymns by the congregation, an Indian stood up and calmly pulled off his shirt, asking to be whipped for his disobedience to the Great Spirit's commands during the past week. "Fourteen stripes were given him by three Indians near by," Hopkins recalled, "with smooth hickory rods about three feet long." The Indian's face was as expressionless as the bravest of warriors, and he withstood the ordeal "without a movement to indicate pain." Fifty other Indians then stepped forward to accept the same punishment, each bearing fourteen or twenty-eight lashes "laid on with such force that any one of them left a mark." After the ceremony the penitents shook hands with their flagellators and returned contentedly to their lodges.[12]

Forgiveness of sin was not the only reason for which Kenekuk appointed men to inflict corporal punishment on wrongdoers. The prophet understood that tribal solidarity was the best insurance against white assaults on his people's lands, possessions, and culture. Faced in the 1820s with the constant threat of expulsion from the Wabash area, Kenekuk and the other leaders employed the whippings to maintain discipline and as an effective means of strengthening tribal unity. They also knew that the violent anti-American policies of Tecumseh and the Shawnee Prophet had been disastrous, and the chiefs were determined that the Vermillion Kickapoos would avoid similar confrontations in the future. Kenekuk hoped that frontier settlers would accept peaceful and sober Indians as neighbors, and he therefore condemned violence and alcoholism. He commanded his followers to turn the other cheek when they were wronged, and he warned drunkards that they would go to hell if they failed to reform. These admonitions proved remarkably effective. During a time when large numbers of Americans, regardless of race, were suffering from the effects of alcoholism, Kenekuk's followers abstained. Their temperance helped to prevent incidents that whites could use as an excuse or justification for attacking or expelling the Indians.

Kenekuk also knew that whites would be more sympathetic if the Indians' religious practices appeared to be like those of other Americans. Because his disciples were not able to read the Bible, the prophet consecrated and sold each of them a "prayer stick"—a narrow twelve–inch walnut or maple board on which three sets of five traditional Kickapoo figures were carved. These represented the owner's heart, life, name, friends, and flesh; above these figures was drawn a picture of an Indian church, standing at the edge of a cornfield. Charles Murray noticed that during a Kickapoo ceremony, each worshiper held "a flat board, on which were carved symbols, which answered the purpose of letters, and enabled

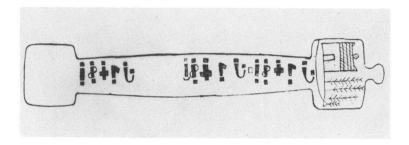

Drawing of a Kickapoo prayer stick showing the markings the Indians "used in prayer like Roman beads." Courtesy of the Kansas State Historical Society.

them to chime in with the prayer or hymn of the preacher." An Illinois settler recalled that the "boards were uniform in size and appearance, and were held very sacred. No Indian thought of retiring for the night without first consulting his board." When an adherent of the prophet died, furthermore, his prayer stick was buried with him.[13]

Outsiders thought that the prayer sticks bore some resemblance to the rosary; indeed, although the Kickapoos and most American Indians considered four their sacred number, the markings on the boards were arranged like the rosary's fifteen mysteries, in three groups of five each.[14] The Indians even manipulated the devices while chanting like Catholics at prayer. The Presbyterian William Smith was fascinated by the "hyeroglyphic characters used in prayer like Roman beads." Isaac McCoy also wondered about the "arbitrary characters, which they followed up with their finger until the last character admonished them that they had completed the prayer." McCoy noticed that the Indians went over each figure several times during a service, all the while chanting "in a monotonous sing-song tone." To him, "the repetitions were exceedingly frequent, almost the same words of

A disciple of the Kickapoo prophet holding a prayer stick. Courtesy of the Thomas Gilcrease Institution of American History and Art.

a short sentence being repeated many times, and all apparently unmeaning."[15]

While meaningless to outsiders such as McCoy, the prayers

held deep significance for the Indians, and the similarities between the teachings of Christianity and Kenekuk's religion should have been evident. But under Kenekuk's astute guidance, the Kickapoos applied their own interpretations to Christian religious practices; they modified and adopted Catholic and Protestant ideas and symbols to form a theology that was distinctly Indian in character. "They are moral in their deportment and seem very sincere in their religion," William Smith told his Presbyterian superiors. "They have heard that a person called Christ lived and died and is now in heaven, but when I inquired the reason of his death, I could discover nothing more than that they had seen a silver cross, which they had been taught to venerate." In Smith's eyes, Kenekuk's followers were definitely not Christians![16]

Although the Kickapoos had put aside the Algonquin medicine bundles that had formerly protected them in their daily lives, had stopped painting their bodies and going to war, and had abandoned many other traditional practices, their religion remained thoroughly in harmony with Indian beliefs. They steadfastly refused to speak English, and they always performed their traditional music and dancing at religious ceremonies. At prayer meetings, moreover, menstruating women were not allowed to participate or go near the place where the "medicine" was kept, indicating that the menstrual taboo was still rigorously enforced. Such practices disturbed many whites, and the Indians' reverence of Kenekuk, instead of a priest or minister, rankled and frustrated the missionaries. William Smith, for one, realized that although the Kickapoo Prophet ruled "in a manner which would reflect honor on an enlightened statesman," his "wholly heathen" teachings "would be impossible to break down."[17]

Smith's analysis was correct, for whites found it difficult if not impossible to counter Kenekuk's teachings, which gave his people the strength and courage to struggle for their rights, as part of the growing nation, and the wisdom to avoid violence against the more powerful Americans. Kenekuk astutely protected the Indians by helping to revitalize their culture and ways. Throughout his life, he effectively resisted efforts by federal officials and missionaries to force his people to profess Christianity or to abandon their lands. His word was not one of rebellion against the United States; his message was peaceful. Despite a hostile and changing environment, his religion kept Indian culture viable. During the first half of the nineteenth century, when many Indians lost their tribal identities, their possessions, and their lands, the Vermillion bands prospered. They owed their survival to Kenekuk, especially to his religious tenets stressing peace, temperance, and land retention, as well as his insistence that men farm the fields—a radical departure from the Indian custom that assigned farming to women. Kenekuk knew why his people endured: "The most of those of my color are foolish and wicked. I have had the good fortune to be instructed by the Great Spirit in a good and correct course."[18] That course proved to be a practical accommodation to white society.

4. Protector of His People's Rights

The Vermillion Kickapoos and their allies faced an uncertain future after the 1819 land-cession treaty. Fortunately, they had a leader who was capable of dealing with most of the crises that arose during the 1820s. Many times the artful Kenekuk maneuvered to circumvent federal and local efforts to evict his people from the Wabash region. On the surface, Kenekuk's course of action seemed obvious: he told whites what they wanted to hear. "You are my brother[s]," he assured them, "the land is yours and we have no claim to it."[1] But while he often promised that his people were about to emigrate beyond the Mississippi, he always found some excuse for not complying, and his followers maintained a tenuous hold on their precious lands to the end of the decade.

Throughout the 1820s, Kenekuk worked to protect his people's rights. In St. Louis on February 10, 1827, for example, he spoke at length to Superintendent of Indian Affairs William Clark about the Kickapoos' desire to remain in the Indiana-Illinois region. The superintendent, the famous explorer of Lewis and Clark fame, was the federal official in charge of Indian affairs for the Mississippi and Missouri rivers region; he negotiated treaties and supervised federal Indian agents in a territory that extended from Indiana to present-day Kansas and Nebraska. The Kickapoo

Prophet had traveled across Illinois to confer with Clark because whites were threatening "to take up the tomahawk" if the Indians continued to delay their emigration.

Kenekuk pleaded with Clark to let the Kickapoos "remain a little longer where we are now." His logic had a compelling simplicity: "My father, you call all the redskins your children. When we have children, we treat them well. That is the reason I make this long talk to get you to take pity on us." Because they had "thrown all [their] badness away and kept the good path," furthermore, they should be allowed to keep their lands. The Indians had begun to follow the white man's road. They had settled down, had planted crops, and were getting along well with their white neighbors. Because the Kickapoos had thrown "their tomahawks aside and put up their hands to the Great Spirit," they were sure to become prosperous again. They needed time to prove that they were worthy members of the American community at large.

Clark listened intently as Kenekuk made his appeal; the superintendent could hardly dispute the arguments of one who insisted that his words came directly from God. "When I talked to the Great Spirit," Kenekuk related, "He did not tell me to sell my lands, because I did not know how much was a dollar's worth, or the game that runs on it. If He told me so, I would tell you today." And since God owned the land, how could mere men buy and sell it? "Some of our chiefs said the land belonged to us, the Kickapoos," Kenekuk continued, "but this is not what the Great Spirit told me— the lands belong to Him. The Great Spirit told me that no people owned the lands—that all was His, and not to forget to tell the white people that when we went into council."

Kenekuk concluded by again asking Clark to treat the Indians fairly; let them remain on the lands of their fathers.

Avoid angering God, he advised his host, for "everything belongs to the Great Spirit. If He chooses to make the earth shake, all the skins, white and red, can not stop it. I have done, I trust to the Great Spirit."[2]

This was only one of Kenekuk's many successful appeals in behalf of his people. Throughout the 1820s, this religious and secular leader of approximately four hundred Indians— about one hundred and fifty of whom were Potawatomi converts—resisted all efforts to move his followers west of the Mississippi. Betrayed by a few greedy "chiefs," the Vermillion people had officially surrendered all claims to their territory in the 1819 treaty, but they loved the Wabash region and did not want to move. The Kickapoos "positively refuse to leave the lands which they now occupy in Illinois," reported an emissary of William Clark's in 1823, "aleging that they had not sold it, nor authorized any person to sell it for them, and would not give it up."[3]

As federal officials increasingly exerted pressure on the Indians to move, the latter relied more and more on the charismatic Kenekuk—the "tall bony Indian, with a keen black eye, and a face beaming with intelligence"—who often traveled to St. Louis to plead the Indians' case.[4] The Kickapoo Prophet's eloquent appeals found favor with the red-headed William Clark, who had championed Indian causes since his famous expedition to the Pacific with Meriwether Lewis in the early 1800s. As long as the Vermillion people remained peaceful, and local politicians and settlers found no pressing justification for removing the Indians, the superintendent would permit them to remain.

Despite Clark's liberal approach toward the Vermillion Kickapoos and other bands, the 1820s and early 1830s proved to be difficult years for eastern Indians. Since the turn of the century, the federal government had pursued a dual policy of obtaining lands for an expanding American nation while attempting to absorb the Indians gradually into mainstream society. But as the years passed, it became apparent that acquiring territory to satisfy the needs of white settlers far outweighed the importance of assimilating the Indians. Because the Indians refused to cultivate the land "as God intended," whites argued, the government had a moral obligation to run the "savages" off.[5] Waving the banner of states' rights, Georgia, Alabama, Mississippi, and other southern states began to clash with the federal government over the jurisdiction of Indians within their borders. State officials argued that the tribes hindered progress, and they demanded that the Indians be removed immediately.

Pressures to evict the tribes also mounted in the Old Northwest. By the 1820s the growing populations of Indiana, Illinois, and Missouri were eager to rid themselves of Indians and to occupy the latter's lands. In Illinois, disagreement and strife characterized relations between the races, with much of the rancor centering on the Prairie Kickapoos. While most of the Prairie Indians emigrated to Missouri shortly after the 1819 treaty at Edwardsville, the followers of Chief Mecina who were living along the Sangamon River refused to leave. Angry that whites were trespassing on their lands, some Prairie Kickapoos began to raid farms and to run off with livestock and other property. In the spring of 1822, a few of them taunted a settler as they passed his house near Vandalia, Illinois, and when they stole some "trifling property," angry citizens gave chase and forcibly recovered the man's belongings.

Such "outrages" induced a delegation of state officials to visit the Prairie Kickapoo villages along the Sangamon, forty-five miles north of Vandalia. The officials found that the Indians had "no hostile designs" toward whites, but the local settlers were still clamoring for the expulsion of the Indians.[6] Along the Wabash in western Indiana, the Vermillion Kickapoos also had allegedly destroyed the property of white settlers; disputes had broken out and violence was threatened; but the Indian Agent John Tipton had settled matters quickly and peacefully. The agent Richard Graham blamed whiskey peddlers for starting most of the trouble with the Kickapoos. "The facility with which whiskey can be introduced among the Indians, renders them very savage [and] ungovernable," he informed Secretary of War Calhoun, "a stop if possible should be put to it, but the law is so lame . . . that an agent can do nothing."[7]

The sympathetic Graham knew that most of Mecina's followers were peaceful and honest and that only a few restless warriors had caused much of the trouble in central Illinois.[8] But he also realized that whether or not the Prairie Kickapoos were hostile, the local settlers were complaining that the Indians had profited little from years of intercourse with white society. Most of the settlers agreed with Maj. Morrell Marston of Fort Harrison that the Indians appeared "to be more apt to learn and practice [whites'] vices, than their virtues." In April 1824 an Illinois citizens' committee petitioned Superintendent Clark to remove the Kickapoos. The Indians had committed several outrages against honest citizens, the petitioners claimed, and this "has been a great hindrance to the settling of . . . the state. The Indians being so numerous in our vicinity that people from a great distance coming to view their lands give up all idea of bringing on their families so long as the Indians continue to reside in our neighborhood and amongst us."[9]

The Kickapoos, in turn, complained that ill-mannered whites were ruining Indian neighborhoods. "Too much come," the frustrated Mecina railed at one point, "back white

man, t'other side Sangamon." The usually good-natured
Mecina warned one intruder that he would burn down the
man's house if the man refused to leave; but the chief's threat
failed, and the white man was left unharmed. Other Prairie
Kickapoos, however, used threats of violence to strike real
fear into the encroachers. "In two moons more," they
predicted in October 1825, "the great man above will rain
down Kickapoos enough to cover all that land." The Indians
would then be powerful enough to expel the unwanted settlers. Alarmed whites implored Illinois' acting governor, A. F.
Hubbard, to do something about the "savages" who were
"killing their hoggs before their eyes and in defiance of the
settlers, declaring the land is theirs and that the whites are
intruders upon it; and that they will fight before they will
leave." Although he evidently doubted the veracity of these
charges, Hubbard beseeched Superintendent Clark to in-
tervene in order to prevent trouble. "It would be highly grati-
fying to our citizens," Hubbard wrote, "that such steps should
be taken as are best calculated to ascertain who are the ag-
gressors the whites or the indians."[10]

Clark had already sent Richard Graham to investigate the
matter, and in January 1825 the agent located Mecina's people
peacefully hunting along the south fork of the Sangamon.
Quickly sizing up the situation, Graham determined that the
settlers' accusations were unfounded. "I have very few complaints of these Indians," he reported, "and could establish
no facts of any depredations which they had committed."

When Graham asked if the Indians intended to abide by
the 1819 treaty and move from Illinois, Mecina responded
indignantly that he had never signed away tribal lands. "I
cannot say this land belongs to me," Mecina admitted, "[but]
I can't say my body belongs to me, it belongs to the Great
Spirit." Those Kickapoos who signed the treaty had violated

sacred laws. "I thought the Great Spirit was mad because there was a shaking of the earth," the chief continued, "and I thought it was because the Red Skins was such fools as to sell their lands. The Great Spirit shook the land after we sold because He was angry, and I am afraid of Him." After conferring with Mecina, Graham concluded that the Kickapoos' love for their homes was so strong that they would leave only at bayonet point.[11]

Kenekuk's followers, who were living in the Wabash bottom near the mouth of Pine Creek, were equally determined never to abandon their homes. Life there was good for the Kickapoos and their allies, because the Indians had many acres of corn, beans, pumpkins, and other crops under cultivation. Deer and other game were still plentiful also, and the stream of clear water that ran through their main village was big and rapid enough to turn a grist mill, which the industrious Indians hoped to build eventually.[12] It was at this village in February 1827 that Graham met with the Kickapoo Prophet, who made quite an impression on the agent. "This man has acquired an influence over his people through supposed revelations from God," Graham noted, "which he urges on them with an eloquence, mildness, and firmness of manner that carries to their credulous ears conviction of his communication with God." Kenekuk's people "neither drank nor painted, were serious, though not gloomy," observed the agent, who doubted if they could ever be induced to move voluntarily.

Kenekuk, who was aware that federal officials were determined to find justification for evicting the Indians, tried to mollify Graham by assuring him that the Kickapoos would soon abandon the Indiana-Illinois region. But first, the prophet would have to talk with God to determine His views on the matter. In the meantime, Kenekuk had much to do in converting "bad men" to the ways of the Great Spirit. Realizing that violence against whites would only hasten the expulsion of the Indians, he promised to continue their good-neighbor policy. During their remaining time in the Wabash area, therefore, the Indians would respect the property of local settlers. Even if whites were to assault an Indian or steal his possessions, that man "would bow his head and not complain; he would stop any attempt to take revenge."[13]

Graham recognized the tactics of delay and later advised Clark that Kenekuk "had no idea of giving up his lands."[14] The sympathetic agent knew, however, that although the Indians remained on good terms with their white neighbors, events beyond the Indians' control had already served to make their removal west of the Mississippi inevitable.

In Washington, President John Quincy Adams, shortly after taking office in 1825, also realized that his administration was facing a moral dilemma concerning eastern Indians. The government's longstanding civilization program had proved embarrassingly successful as the Cherokees, Creeks, Potawatomis, Vermillion Kickapoos, and several other eastern bands had taken on the trappings of white society. Because they were peaceful and industrious, Adams had no reasonable grounds to justify forced removal. But because of pressures from politicians in the South and in the Old Northwest, the president adopted a policy of strongly urging the tribes to move.

Impatient state officials from Georgia to Missouri were not satisfied with Adams's mild approach; they demanded immediate federal action. Indiana's Governor James Ray, for example, wrote Adams in November 1825 that the Indians controlled far too much valuable land and asked for help in pressuring the tribes to leave. Ray even went so far as to insinuate that the "most enlightened" tribal elders wanted to emigrate because alcoholism was causing a "visible degeneracy" among the young. They must move for their own good, he argued, for it "is evident that the use which they make of their money, in purchasing spirituous liquors and using them to such great excess as they do, under no moral restraint whatever, will be the most effectual method of extinguishing their race."

The governor made no mention of the fact that the Kickapoos and others living along the Wabash practiced abstinence, or that white citizens got drunk and rowdy as often as did the Indians. His intentions were clear; he would use any means at his disposal—excuses, even threats and lies—to get rid of the tribes. "I would feel proud," he sanctimoniously informed the president, "if consistent with your feelings, to have it in my power to make an effort, during the next season, to extinguish this [Indian] title."[15]

Even most members of the relatively moderate Adams administration agreed that the eastern Indians should move for their own well-being. On January 28, 1826, in response to Ray's demands, Secretary of War James Barbour announced that the president was ready to cooperate with state officials in removing the Indians. Expressing the prevailing sentiment among federal officials, Barbour wrote that there was "but one opinion in regard to the perishing effects which are felt by an Indian population when located in the midst of civilized people. Corruption and fraud, those active agents . . . lead to their degeneracy and impoverishment, and finally to their destruction."[16]

The irresponsible actions of "civilized" whites, more than anything else, however, were what led to the eventual dispossession of the eastern tribes. Between the Rock and the Mississippi rivers in western Illinois the Sacs, Foxes, Winnebagoes, and others (including some Prairie Band Kickapoos), grew restless as rowdy white squatters began to invade their lands. Unscrupulous traders plied Indians with whiskey, then robbed them of their possessions. Occasional violence erupted between drunken Indians and whites, innocent bystanders were assaulted, and both groups retaliated for hostile acts.

Illinois' Governor Ninian Edwards seized this opportunity to rid his state of Indians, and on August 20, 1827, he called out the militia "to defend our frontiers." Making an enormous issue out of a smattering of isolated minor incidents, the governor warned that a full-scale outbreak was imminent. "I need scarcely remark to you what all experience has proved," Edwards wrote the secretary of war, "that whenever the Indians have once made up their minds to commit hostilities, or have actually committed such, as deserve chastisement, then pacific dispositions never can be safely relied on till they have begged for peace, and begged it so earnestly, as to leave no doubt of their sincerity."[17]

The Indians had, in fact, no intention whatever of going on the warpath, as Edwards undoubtedly realized. But he used the pretext of impending attack to warn officials in Washington that he would use any means at his disposal to expel the tribes from Illinois. When federal officials ignored his obvious cries of "wolf," the governor complained bitterly that the Indian presence "has been borne by the people for a few years past with great impatience, and can not be submitted to much longer." The Indians must be removed "with as little delay as possible."[18]

President Adams, although he was generally sympathetic to Edwards's call for removal, moved slowly. His administration was already smarting from verbal attacks by angry Georgians and other southerners, but Adams also wanted to avoid angering his New England allies—the backbone of his political strength—by using force on the peaceful eastern tribes. He therefore instructed Secretary of War Barbour to take a cautious approach to the situation in Illinois, "consistent with humanity."

In response, the annoyed Edwards wrote to the secretary of war in October 1827, insisting that Indians who had ceded their lands through treaty—which included the Chippewas, Delawares, Potawatomis, Ottawas, Sacs, Foxes, and Kickapoos—must go at once. He pointed out that the eastern states did not allow "red savages" to roam about, depleting game and disturbing the peace. The people of Illinois, therefore, should not "be expected to permit large bands of marauding savages, without any right whatever, to be constantly traversing this State, for the total destruction of our [wild game]." Requiring the Kickapoos and others to abide by their treaties, Edwards insisted, was a moral obligation that the federal government must carry out with all due speed.[19]

Because of Edwards's complaints, William Clark ordered agent Graham to confer again with the Kickapoos and to warn them about "the consequences likely to result on their refusing or neglecting to remove next spring." But in carrying out his orders that November, Graham discovered that almost all of the Prairie Kickapoos had already left Illinois; only Mecina and his most ardent followers were still living and hunting along the Sangamon, Illinois, and Kaskaskia rivers. This intractable faction, he noted, seemed "determined not to leave the land of [their] fathers." He also found that Kenekuk and his people were still opposed to removal, and much to the chagrin of local authorities, their activities were now centered in a triangular region between the Vermillion and Mackinaw rivers, from Danville northwest to present-day Pontiac and south to modern Bloomington, Illinois.[20]

The agent undoubtedly realized that his mission was futile. The Indians trusted him and believed that he, as well as Superintendent Clark, had the Indians' best interests at heart; the agent knew, therefore, that his less-than-enthusiastic words of warning would fall on deaf ears. But despite mixed feelings, he carried out his orders on November 23. "The Great Chief of the white people on whose lands you are now hunting," he announced through his interpreter, Pierre Menard, "complains to your Great Father [the president] that you are in his way—and if you do not go away some injury might be done to you." The Kickapoos, after all, had signed a land-cession treaty, and their refusal to leave was not justified. "Do not shut your eyes to what I am now telling you. If a blind man falls, he is to be pitied, but if a man who can see falls, no one pities him,—take this caution and do not run your wives and children into any distress with the white people." The federal government, moreover, would no longer rush to the rescue if settlers tried to evict the Indians forcibly. "It has been only your Great Father's arm that has restrained the white people from driving you off before now," Graham reminded the Indians, "he will not hold it back any longer; he says you must go—he will not listen any longer to your talk, asking to let you stay another year."[21]

The overconfident Superintendent Clark had already informed Secretary of War Barbour that all of the Indians now residing on ceded Illinois lands would be gone by spring. Clark was under the mistaken impression that the Kickapoos had refused to relocate in Missouri before then because of jealousy and bad blood between the Prairie and Vermillion bands. Their quarrelsomeness would soon be resolved, he reckoned. "The Prophet, a Kickapoo Indian of considerable note among them, is now using every exertion to quiet their jealousies hindering them to move."[22]

Kenekuk was indeed trying to establish friendlier relations with the Prairie Band, but hardly for the reasons that Clark thought. The prophet knew that if his followers were to join with Mecina's, the combined bands could present a united front against removal. Kenekuk also recognized that both he and Mecina held the same convictions against selling Indian lands and possessions, and the prophet therefore endeavored to persuade the remaining Prairie Kickapoos to embrace his religion.

The major obstacle to the plan lay in the adherence of Mecina's people to traditional ways. Their far-lesser degree of acculturation was illustrated early in 1828, when the Prairie Indians staged a traditional Kickapoo dance near present-day Bloomington, Illinois, for the benefit of the white settlers. Jeremiah Rhodes, one of the settlers, recalled that twenty gallons of whiskey were on hand for the ceremony and that one drunken Indian later beat his wife over the head with a bottle. Rhodes also saw six or eight dancers with their bodies painted black and a pair of crossed arms and hands painted on their chests. At the climax of the dance a brave pointed "a stick cut in the shape of a gun" up to the sky, while others brandished tomahawks.

The ceremonial music, which held deep religious significance for all Kickapoos, was performed in typical Indian fashion. Their intonations were so off key and inconsistent to white ears that listeners such as Rhodes found it monotonous; the instruments served mainly a percussive function and seemed not to be coordinated with the singing. Rhodes noted that the men continually sang the words "hu way, hu way," while Mecina shook a stone-filled gourd, and a youth beat a drum—a ten-gallon keg with an animal skin drawn over one end. The young John Dawson, also in attendance, thought that the Indian music lacked rhythm

and melody—"no other race ever called such howls singing"—as he watched his father join in the merrymaking.
When the elder Dawson began to sing, however, the
Kickapoos quickly put a stop to it. "No sing, friend Dawson,
just dance," pleaded Mecina. Either Dawson's singing voice
was too terrible for even the kind-hearted Mecina to bear,
or the chief did not want a white man singing religious
songs.[23]

Soon after this ceremony, Mecina and many of his people
abandoned their haunts along the Sangamon and went east
to join the prophet. The Vermillion people readily welcomed
their Prairie Kickapoo brothers and sisters, because Mecina's
people already adhered to similar beliefs and principles.
Some, including Mecina, had even converted to Kenekuk's
religion; their gun-shaped sticks, which they told whites were
symbols of peace, were undoubtedly the prophet's prayer
sticks. The blades of the tomahawks used in their ceremonies were always covered by firm hands, moreover, a sign
that the bearers harbored no violent intentions. Although
many still occasionally drank to excess and acted improperly, they were ready to seek accord with the whites, and they
asked Kenekuk to show them the way.

The prophet was happy to accommodate his Prairie
Kickapoo friends, because he needed their help in staving
off the forces arrayed for removing them from Illinois. He
had to act quickly, for his people were expected to move to
Missouri in that spring of 1828. In May, determined to keep
their lands and to disprove Governor Edwards's charges of
Indian misconduct, Kenekuk and twenty of his followers
began the 190-mile trek to St. Louis to confer with Superintendent Clark. Arriving on Saturday, May 17, the Indians
settled into a local hotel, where the Kickapoo Prophet
gathered his thoughts for the conference on the following

day.[24] Perhaps Clark would still have mercy and not force them to abandon the lands of their fathers. Kenekuk could only wonder: "How long . . . will our women and children be permitted to live in quietness in this land?"

The Kickapoo Prophet entered the superintendent's office that Sunday, confident that the Great Spirit sided with the Indians in their quest to keep their homes. "My brother! You know those of my color are poor and have not the means of living as happy as the white people," he told Clark. "You appear to have some foreknowledge of that which may happen, perhaps 'tis from God and I hope it will prevent us from becoming more poor." It was the Sabbath, and Kenekuk had come prepared with a forceful speech. Lifting his hands toward heaven, he swore that his people had not committed any wrongful acts against the whites. Perhaps Governor Edwards was lying, Kenekuk intoned. Indeed, his people were no threat to their neighbors—quite the opposite. "To be sure sometimes the whites kill our dogs," he admitted, "but we pass on and never mind it." In one instance a gang of white ruffians had assaulted one of the Kickapoo chiefs, Kenekuk related. After striking the chief with their rifles, they had stolen eighty deer skins and burned his wickiup. Despite such injustices, the Kickapoos had remained peaceful and wanted to stay in Illinois for at least another year. Turning to Clark, the prophet remarked: "Brother! When you last spoke to me everything appeared smooth—now there appears to be trouble."[25]

When Clark's turn finally came to reply, he warned the prophet that attacks on the Indians would continue as long as they lived on the Vermillion. "You will be involved in brawls with the whites, owing to the restless disposition of some of your people and ours," the superintendent predicted; "for this reason it would be better for you to have land without the boundaries of the state, where you will never be interrupted."

Kenekuk understood history too well to be swayed by such platitudes. Time and again the United States government had reneged on its promises to the Indians. Why should it be any different now? Those Kickapoos who had settled along the Osage River in Missouri, moreover, were already facing intense pressure to move farther west. Another year, he beseeched Clark—one year to make final preparations for any move:

> My brother! I know there are chiefs above you, and 'tis for this reason that I fear when things go wrong. I also fear to disobey the directions of the Great Spirit by abandoning what I have undertaken at His command before the expiration of the time I mention. My father, I speak the truth, as I fear the Great Spirit—and I wish to do a good and solid business when we do move. When all matters between nations shall be arranged and when peace and harmony is restored, then we can be settled, and there will be no poor among us.
>
> My brother! What I have said has relieved my heart—the sun shines, for all is clear, and I hope the Great Spirit will hear what is said here today.[26]

After the conference, Kenekuk remained in St. Louis for a few days. He knew that the Great Spirit had heard his pleas, but he wanted to make sure that the white people were listening as well. He played upon their sympathies, admitting that they were right—the land legally belonged to them. But whites should realize that abandoning Illinois would only hurt the Indians—a people striving to live by God's commands. "I raise my hands every day to the Great Spirit," the prophet told St. Louis audiences, "for I wish to act correctly and induce the people of my nation to abandon their vices." He hoped that the citizens of Illinois would not insist upon removal, for the final decision in the matter lay in their hands. The Indians' ultimate fate, however, rested with the Great Spirit. "If I do not act agreeably to His will, He will reduce us to nothing and finally destroy our nation."[27]

William Clark was perplexed, for he had seemingly exhausted every means of persuading the Kickapoos to move voluntarily. The superintendent was an honorable man, and he sympathized with the Indians. He understood their love for their lands, and he found Kenekuk's compelling arguments against removal "very sensible." Clark had little doubt that the Kickapoo Prophet, although "touched as usual with the colours of his fancy, and mysteriously variegated by his divinity," was a good influence on his followers. Clark decided, therefore, to let the peaceful and unobtrusive Indians stay in the Vermillion River area a while longer.[28]

Ninian Edwards was outraged when he heard the news. On May 29 the livid Illinois governor gave notice that if Clark failed to act soon, the state militia would evict the Kickapoos by force. "I trust you must see the necessity of substituting force for persuasion," he warned Clark. The federal government's failure to remove the band, moreover, was "an invasion of the rights of a sovereign and independent State, and therefore were the President himself to assent to the request of the Kickapoo Prophet and his party to remain another year at their present village it would not be submitted to." His "outrageously harassed" state was determined to rid itself of the "savages," Edwards stormed; "if any act of hostility shall be committed on the frontier, I shall not hesitate to remove them on my own responsibility."[29]

Such pompous exhortations had little effect on Clark. He

knew that Edwards was an astute politician who employed Indian-hating rhetoric in order to drum up support from the voting public but that the governor lacked sufficient military means to carry out his threats. Ignoring Edwards's harangues, Clark wrote to his superiors in Washington on June 1, 1828, that most Indians would leave Illinois during the course of that summer. The only exception would be Kenekuk's band, "the most orderly and sober Indians within the State of Illinois."[30]

The Adams administration, thinking ahead to the presidential election that fall, tried to mollify Edwards as well as Illinois voters. Secretary of War Peter B. Porter assured the governor on July 7 that every means would be taken to hasten the removal of the Kickapoos and other stragglers. The Indians, Porter noted, were an inherently slow-moving people, and it would be "best to indulge them." Porter implored Edwards to be patient; Kenekuk, after all, had "pledged" to remove his people by May of the following year. "Their claims upon our forbearance and liberality," the secretary wrote, "will not I am sure be least upon your Excellency who knows so well the nature of those relations which exist between us, and those unfortunate people."[31]

The administration's moderate approach to Indian removal, however, satisfied neither Governor Edwards nor Illinois voters. Most agreed with Isaac McCoy, a Baptist missionary from Indiana who was a staunch advocate of removal and had gained nationwide influence by the late 1820s. McCoy proposed to establish a separate Indian state or colony outside the limits of the American states and territories. In such an isolated colony, missionaries such as himself could help to resettle, educate, and Christianize the relocated tribes. With this in mind, McCoy secured permission from Commissioner of Indian Affairs Thomas McKenney to search for a suitable territory and, in August 1828, McCoy led a party to the lands directly west of the Missouri state line.

McCoy was pleasantly surprised by what he found in what is now eastern Kansas. For seventy-five miles past the Missouri border, there was enough timber to support "a tolerably dense population," the soil was fertile; and there was enough water. A return visit a short time later convinced him that he had found his "Indian Canaan." But for his dream to become reality, the federal government had to make Indian removal mandatory, and that meant abandoning the Adams administration's cautious approach. Force was necessary; the well-being of the Indians was at stake. Willingly or not, they must be removed for their own good![32]

As the 1828 presidential election approached, the appeal of candidate Andrew Jackson became irresistible to the advocates of Indian removal. General Jackson had been their hero ever since his dramatic victory over the Creeks during the War of 1812. "Old Hickory" seemed to be a man of the people—a western slaveholder, a hater of the national banks as well as aristocrats, a nationalist, but also an upholder of states' rights—the direct opposite of the intellectual and compassionate Adams. Citizens of Ohio, Indiana, Illinois, Missouri, and the South realized that his sympathies lay with white settlers against the Indians, and whites flocked to vote for him. With Jackson in office, they knew that the fertile but unexploited Indian lands would soon be opened, and when only New England voters supported the incumbent, a Democratic landslide was assured. The election result proved to be a harbinger of bad times to come for eastern Indians such as the Kickapoos and their allies. The new Jackson administration had plans to push all of them west of the Mississippi with as little delay as possible.

Along the Vermillion River in eastern Illinois, however,

Kenekuk's followers remained unconcerned, for they had "opened their hands and [thrown] away all their vices and bad thoughts." Surely the new "father" in Washington would allow them to remain on their lands. There was little to fear after all, for their prophet had placed his trust in the Great Spirit and his fellow man. "Every red and white man is my brother," Kenekuk often explained, "and I desire to be united with them in [friendship], and for this reason I am afraid of nothing."[33]

5. The Storms of War and Removal

The spring of 1829 passed, and Kenekuk's followers still clung to their precious lands in eastern Illinois. Despite his promises to move by May of that year, the Kickapoo Prophet had no intention of ever taking his people west. His compelling arguments against removal had touched the heart of William Clark, who was impressed by the prophet's efforts to bring Kickapoo customs in line with white ways. White settlers in the Vermillion River region were also somewhat taken with Kenekuk, whom they esteemed as a "correct, pious, and excellent man." They knew that the prophet was "much attached to the whites" and that he had "acquired an astonishing influence over his red brethren and has induced all of his particular tribe . . . to abstain entirely from the use of ardent spirits."[1] The whites willingly accepted these sober and peaceful Indians as neighbors. Even Illinois state officials toned down their demands for the expropriation of the Kickapoos, which eased the pressure for removal temporarily. But the sun that shone and warmed the hearts of Indians and whites in Illinois was soon to be eclipsed, for the clouds of war arose on the western horizon.

Along the Rock and Mississippi rivers in western Illinois, events were unfolding that would greatly affect Kenekuk's peaceful followers and end their hope of remaining in Illinois. The Sacs and Foxes of the Mississippi, as they were known, had lived in this region for generations and insisted that they would never abandon it. An 1804 land-cession treaty, however, called for their eventual removal to Iowa, but as the Indians pointed out, the officials had negotiated that agreement with "chiefs" who had no right to speak for the tribes. By the late 1820s the Sacs and Foxes were still resolutely clinging to their lands, vowing to drive all white intruders from their territory.[2]

When the Sacs and Foxes left for their winter hunt in 1828, however, rumors abounded in the nearby white settlements that the Indians had left forever. Assuming that they had submitted to William Clark's general order to leave Illinois by May of the following year, large numbers of white squatters rushed in to stake claims; the unruly trespassers trampled the Indians' cornfields and destroyed their lodges. When the Sacs and Foxes returned in early 1829, they were surprised and angered by the destruction. They did their best to carry on, however, occupying their remaining lodges and planting new patches of corn. For a while the situation was explosive, and violence occasionally broke out that spring and summer between whites and the followers of a Sac warrior named Black Hawk.[3]

In Washington, meanwhile, a storm of a different kind was brewing, for the Jackson administration had set in motion plans to push all of the remaining eastern tribes beyond the Mississippi.[4] Shortly after taking office, the new president assured doubters that he did not intend to abuse Indian rights: "You may be rest assured that I shall adhere to the just and humane policy towards the Indians." Jackson continued:

In this spirit I have recommended them to quit their possessions on this side of the Mississippi, and go to a country to
the west where there is every probability that they will always
be free from the mercenary influence of white men, and un-
disturbed by the local authority of the states: Under such
circumstances the General Government can exercise a parental
control over their interests and possibly perpetuate their race.[5]

In the South, members of the Five Civilized Tribes asserted
that they had already reached maturity as a people and no
longer needed the "great father's" guidance; they resolutely
opposed all attempts to evict them from their ancestral lands.
"I am sorry I cannot comply with the request of my father,"
one chief stated. "We wish to remain here, where we have
grown up as the herbs of the woods; and do not wish to be
transplanted into another soil."[6] But because Georgia,
Alabama, and Mississippi had already passed laws of questionable constitutionality assuming state jurisdiction over
the Cherokees, Choctaws, Creeks, and other tribes, President Jackson ignored the Indian protests and acted quickly
to appease southern voters.

Hoping to win national support for an aggressive removal
policy, Jackson immediately asked the popular Thomas
McKenney—one of John Quincy Adams's appointees—to
continue as head of the Indian Office. Truly concerned for
the welfare of the tribes, McKenney was considered an ex-
pert on Indian affairs; and politicians, religious leaders, and
newspaper editors respected his views. He firmly believed that
the civilization and Christianization of the Indians could best
be carried out west of the Mississippi under the auspices of
Protestant missionaries.[7]

McKenney accepted the president's offer and quickly set

out to win support for a national Indian-removal law. "Seeing as I do the condition of these people, and that they are bordering on destruction," he told audiences, "I would, were I empowered, take them firmly but kindly by the hand, and tell them they must go." He would do this, he continued, "on the same principle I would take my own children by the hand, firmly but kindly and lead them from a district of the country in which the plague was raging."[8] In order to "save" the Indians from destruction, McKenney and a group of eastern philanthropists organized the New York Board for the Emigration, Preservation and Improvement of the Aborigines of America, which became the chief publicizer of governmental removal propaganda. The organization won considerable support from concerned citizens throughout the country.[9]

Several missionaries, including the Baptist Isaac McCoy, actively supported the removal campaign.[10] In May 1829, McCoy began an eight-month tour of the eastern states to rally the public to embrace the cause. The condition of eastern Indians, McCoy warned listeners, "is becoming more and more miserable every year. I repeat it, *they are positively perishing.*"[11] Indians must be removed immediately, because contact with lower-class whites had hindered their social development. In the West, the Indians would be free of white "vices" and other harmful influences and, under the tutelage of McCoy and his fellow missionaries, would quickly become assimilated Americans.[12]

President Jackson agreed, insisting that his removal program was the only humane solution to a regrettable problem: "Toward the aborigines of the country no one can indulge a more friendly feeling than myself, or would go further in attempting to reclaim them from their wandering habits." Conveniently ignoring the fact that many eastern tribes had highly complex social structures and had long since ceased "wandering," he asked for help in opening "the eyes of those children of the forest to their true condition" so that they would agree to move.[13] The president's strategy should have been clear even to zealous advocates of the program: by referring to Indians as savage children of the wilderness, he was helping to ease the consciences of many whites who recognized his policy for what it really was—a callous device for taking valuable land away from the tribes. Once the Indians were in the West, he assured doubters, the missionaries "may endeavor to teach [the Indians] the arts of civilization, to raise up to an interesting commonwealth, destined to perpetuate the race and to attest the humanity and justice of this government."[14]

For more than a year, similar paternalistic claptrap emanated from the White House. Then, in 1830, congressional debate on a formal removal bill began in earnest. Despite opposition from several missionary groups and New England politicians, Congress wasted little time in approving the legislation. In late April the Indian Removal bill got through the Senate; the House passed the measure by a small margin the following month. On May 28 the president signed into law an act that would open to white settlement "large tracts of country now occupied by a few savage hunters." The Indians would receive lands outside the present states and territories; the government, of course, would provide financial assistance and protection to those who emigrated; and officials insisted that the new lands were guaranteed forever to the relocated tribes. Jackson announced that the new law would free Indians "to cast off their savage habits, and become an interesting, civilized, and Christian community" outside the limits of the United States.[15]

At the Indian Office, Thomas McKenney promised that

the removed tribes would not "be left to roam at large, after arriving in the Country West of the Mississippi. There they should have houses and fields, and workshops; Schools and teachers; a Government, and laws formed expressly for their use—and the future should never be permitted to become to them the source of that calamity which has characterized the past."[16] Both McKenney and the president ignored the fact that many eastern Indians, including the Vermillion Kickapoos, were already enjoying these advantages and did not want to surrender them for an uncertain future in the West.

To appease their tattered consciences, congressmen and federal officials agreed that treaties must be negotiated before removing any tribe; forcing unwilling Indians off their legally owned lands was, after all, immoral. The subsequent treaty process, of course, had exactly the same result, because the government had no intention of negotiating honorably. Federal commissioners and agents resorted to deception, threats, bribery, and other dishonest methods; they avoided legitimate Indian leaders who were opposed to removal and signed land-cession agreements with "paper chiefs"; and then they claimed that the agreements were binding on all. Both the president and McKenney turned deaf ears to the cries of fraud and corruption that arose in Indian country and blandly insisted that all was well; they openly condoned bribery as a proper means to achieve good ends. "All we can do," McKenney insisted, "is advise these people, who at best as a people, are nothing but children, and ought to be treated as such."[17]

Parsimony and incompetence marked the government's handling of the actual removal process, and the Indians suffered severely as a consequence. When administrators awarded contracts for food and transportation to the lowest bidder, many Indian emigrants faced hunger and exposure on their westward exodus, and hundreds died. On their tearful journey west, the Creeks, for example, were fed meat from "some very bad cattle, such as old bulls, and old oxen that were broken down, and not fit either to work or to kill." As one federal official admitted later: "The rivalry of bidding, experience everywhere has shown, induces men, in the heat of the moment, to offer to furnish articles of a given quality lower than they can buy them; and, to make amends for this false step, resort is had to an effort to impose upon the [Indian] department articles, which sometimes may succeed."[18]

All of this mattered little to most Americans; the Indian question was settled to the satisfaction of those who were clamoring for tribal lands, as well as those who believed that removal was the first step toward civilization. President Jackson expressed the general attitude:

> The States which had so long been retarded in their improve-
> ment by the Indian tribes residing in the midst of them are at
> length relieved from the evil, and this unhappy race—the origi-
> nal dwellers in our land—are now placed in a situation where
> we may well hope that they will share in the blessings of civiliza-
> tion and be saved from that degradation and destruction to
> which they were rapidly hastening while they remained in the
> States; and while the safety and comfort of our citizens have
> been greatly promoted by their removal, the philanthropist will
> rejoice that the remnant of that ill-fated race has been at length
> placed beyond the reach of injury or oppression, and that the
> paternal care of the General Government will hereafter watch
> over them and protect them.[19]

News of the removal law set off rejoicing throughout the South and the Old Northwest, for it meant fertile Indian lands would soon be on the market. The settlers of the prosperous state of Illinois were especially optimistic. By the time that John Reynolds succeeded Ninian Edwards as governor in 1830, the frontier wilderness that had existed after the War of 1812 had disappeared; the state's population had increased from forty thousand to almost a quarter of a million; steamboats were plying the Mississippi, Illinois, and Wabash rivers; and Chicago would soon emerge as a bustling lake port. With more settlers arriving every day, the Reynolds administration drew up plans for the evacuation of the state's few remaining Indian tribes.

In 1831, however, the Vermillion Kickapoos and their allies still had no intention of ever abandoning their Illinois lands. Despite the removal law, Kenekuk had successfully resisted every attempt to evict his people. Many times this master of delay had promised to leave, but he always found some last-minute excuse for not complying with official orders to move. Because his followers were friendly and peaceful, moreover, the local settlers did not press the issue. The Indians even began to win a favorable reputation after residents of Danville, Illinois, a short distance from their villages, got permission from Kenekuk to attend one of his services.

When the white citizens arrived at the Indian camp on July 17, 1831, they found that straw mats had been placed on the ground for their comfort. They were guests of honor, and Kenekuk intended to stir their sympathies. Through an interpreter, the prophet advised his audience to beware, for God knows even "the smallest transactions of your lives." All people, he proclaimed, should follow the example set by his Indians: lead good lives, keep God's will, and obey the commandments! "My friends, where are your thoughts today? where were they yesterday? were they fixed upon doing good? or were you drunk, tattling, or did anger rest in

A Kickapoo woman holding her prayer stick. Courtesy of the Thomas Gilcrease Institute of American History and Art.

your hearts?" Turning to his white guests, he proclaimed that the Kickapoos were now walking the righteous path:

> They do not drink strong liquors as they once did; they do not shake their fists at you and abuse you; they do not quar-

rel with each other. Their thoughts are upon their great Father [God]; they are not liars and tattlers, fond of ridiculing old folks and children as they used to be; their conduct toward their children is different. For a long time they have refrained from the bad practices of stealing and drunkenness; their great Father will receive them into His own place where they will be happy; they will never hunger nor thirst; there they will see their children around them; their great Father loves their hearts, for they are strong. Why then should they not love Him? He tells them He loves them; He has given them an opportunity to know Him; the great Father has instilled into them a knowledge of good and evil by His works; He has not instructed them by books.

Concluding an hour-long homily that deeply impressed the visitors, Kenekuk reminded them that God did not discriminate; the Great Spirit "loves His children, both red and white."[20]

When whites found that Kenekuk's people were God-fearing rural folk like themselves, they began to view traditional Kickapoo customs and ways as harmless curiosities instead of as things to fear. Illinois settlers and the Indians began to interact more frequently; visiting, trading, exchanging ideas, and helping each other, the two groups developed a spirit of sharing that was characteristic of many nineteenth-century American farming communities. Settlers such as young William Hendrix of nearby Bloomington paid frequent visits to their Kickapoo neighbors. "Have been at the Indians' camp many times," Hendrix wrote years later, "and the old squaws used to treat me to wild strawberries and wild blackberries. They used to gather the berries and dry them, and they always had an abundance of them dried, and they used to make maple sugar and would also treat me to that." Hendrix and others noticed that, like themselves, the

A Kickapoo man, perhaps a follower of the Prairie Kickapoo leader, Mecina. Courtesy of the Thomas Gilcrease Institute of American History and Art.

Kickapoos planted fields of corn, melons, and tobacco; they gathered nuts, berries, and acorns and collected honey. Although the Indians were still wearing their traditional buckskins, breechcloths, and Mackinaw blankets, along with hats, shirts, and other articles of white clothing, the lo-

cal settlers more readily noted the similarities between themselves and the Indians and played down the insignificant
differences.[21]

The Kickapoos' acceptance was enhanced during those
days when the noted artist George Catlin arrived and painted
portraits of several of them. The artist found Kenekuk "a
very shrewd and talented man" and was pleasantly surprised
and awed by his powerful influence over the Indians. "I
went on the Sabbath to hear this eloquent man preach, when
he had his people assembled in the woods," Catlin wrote later,
"and although I could not understand his language, I was
surprised and pleased with the natural ease and emphasis,
and gesticulation, which carried their own evidence of the
eloquence of his sermon." The sober and peaceful conduct
of the Kickapoos also impressed Catlin, who mistakenly
believed that Kenekuk practiced Christianity. "I was singu-
larly struck with the noble efforts of this champion of the
mere remnant of a poisoned race," the artist recalled, "so
strenuously labouring to rescue the remainder of his people
from the deadly bane [whiskey] that has been brought
amongst them by enlightened Christians." During a rather
lengthy stay, Catlin did not see any of Kenekuk's "zealous
disciples" drink liquor or act improperly. Despite their
"civilized" ways, however, Catlin predicted that they would
"soon be obliged to sell out their country for a trifle, and
move to the West."[22]

In western Illinois, meanwhile, most Sacs and Foxes had
given in to the inevitable and agreed to abide by the removal
treaty. Following the advice of Chief Keokuk, who advised
peaceful accommodation with the whites, these Indians left
their homes along the Rock and Mississippi rivers for lands
in Iowa. By the spring of 1831, only the followers of Black
Hawk remained to face the wrath of the whites who were

determined to drive them "dead or alive over to the west side of the Mississippi." Black Hawk, who had fought alongside the British during the War of 1812, was well known for his anti-American views. He had frequently denounced the treaty that called for the removal of his people from Illinois, and he was now prepared to take a stand.

Governor Reynolds warned federal officials to remove Black Hawk's Sacs and Foxes immediately, or the governor would order the state militia to "exterminate all Indians who will not let us alone." In an effort to avoid bloodshed, Gen. Edmund P. Gaines intervened, and in June he pressured the reluctant Black Hawk and his followers to leave Illinois and join their kinsfolk across the Mississippi.[23]

Unfortunately, the Indians stayed in their new homes for less than a year before Black Hawk led over one thousand homesick men, women, and children back to their old Rock River villages. Included among them were about one hundred Prairie Band Kickapoos (they may have been disaffected members of Mecina's old band who had refused to join with Kenekuk).[24] The Indians, who realized that violence against whites was foolhardy, resettled peacefully and began to plant corn. Despite their peaceful intentions—the women and children would not be accompanying a war party—their return touched off panic among Illinois settlers, and Governor Reynolds requested military assistance from President Jackson. The Illinois state militia, meanwhile, took immediate action to drive the "intruders" back across the Mississippi.

Violence between Black Hawk's people and whites erupted in May 1832. At first, confusion reigned, as both sides were ill prepared to fight. Although the militia troops were undisciplined and lacked field experience, they chased Black Hawk's followers north into Wisconsin and virtually an-

The Kickapoo Prophet. George Catlin most likely added the face paint and feathers to this portrait well after his actual encounter with the Kickapoos. Courtesy of the Thomas Gilcrease Institute of American History and Art.

nihilated the undermanned and poorly armed warriors that August near the mouth of the Bad Axe River. A Kickapoo woman testified later that Black Hawk wanted to avoid bloodshed and that he had tried to negotiate with the soldiers before the final battle. "I take pity on the women and children," the chief reportedly announced; "I will shake hands with the Americans and save you." His efforts were in vain, however, and the Sacs, Foxes, Prairie Kickapoos, and others were easily defeated.[25] The storm of violence that Kenekuk and other peaceful men worked to avoid had run its course. All Indians, even the peaceful Vermillion people, would pay a heavy price, for the war had aroused hysteria among settlers from Missouri to Indiana.

Cries rang out for the immediate removal of all remaining eastern Indians. Reacting to false reports that the Vermillion Kickapoos had participated in the war, the *Vandalia Whig and Illinois Intelligencer* demanded that federal officials act quickly to expel them. "Parties of Kickapoos . . . have been strolling about for some time past, with apparent unconcern, in the country around the headwaters of the Illinois, professing friendship, and pretending to be retreating from the scene of the war," the editors claimed. But "Indians never forget their cunning; our citizens should be cautious of trusting to their professions in whatever shape they come." The *St. Louis Beacon* was even more inflammatory: "Shall the blood of mothers, daughters, and little children, yet fresh on the ground, implore the assistance and invoke the retaliatory vengeance of their friends and fellow citizens in vain?" Sweet revenge! an eye for an eye! the editors screamed. "The blood of the murdered victims of Indian ferocity can admit but one atonement;—the lives of a hundred Indians is too small for that of each of their fallen victims."[26]

On August 19, 1832, Gen. Winfield Scott, the commander of the troops who defeated Black Hawk's warriors, attempted to dispel rumors that Kenekuk's followers were guilty of any violence. "As far as I can learn, the Kickapoos, who have taken part against us, had resided with Black Hawk for several years," Scott informed Secretary of War Lewis Cass. "Several lodges of this tribe broke off & returned to the Wabash, before actual hostilities commenced." In the midst of the crisis, the Indian agent William Marshall had even given Kenekuk's people permission to hunt on federal lands in Illinois, as long as they continued to act "peaceably and amicably." Indeed, the peace-loving Kenekuk would never permit his followers to engage in violence of any kind. His mistake was in providing a haven for refugees from Black Hawk's camp, because panicky whites would ever be suspicious of the "true" motivation that rested behind his act of kindness.

Despite official assurances from General Scott and others that the Vermillion Kickapoos were innocent, citizen demands for their removal intensified. The whites were indignant, even in Indiana, where the *St. Joseph Beacon* had attempted to restore calm by pointing out that there was "no more probability of an invasion by Black Hawk's party than there is from the Emperor of Russia."[27]

By the end of the month, the effects of Jackson's removal law and the shock of the Black Hawk War had begun to overwhelm the Vermillion Indians' valiant effort to remain in Illinois. On August 31, William Clark advised the Kickapoo Prophet to seize "this opportunity of leaving a country where you have long been looked upon with suspicion, and where you will shortly be treated as enemies." The superintendent told Kenekuk that he hoped "the Great Spirit will open your ears to my advice and enable you to act with prudence." The white man assured the skeptical Indian leader that although Clark himself had never personally inspected the new land in the West, he knew it was ideal for resettlement: "Your Great Father, the President, does not wish your people to be permanently placed on land incapable of supporting them comfortably. He wishes to see his Red Children contented and happy. But your people will lose nothing by removing to the country assigned to them."[28]

Kenekuk, who had listened to such empty promises many times before, knew they meant nothing; but with Governor Reynolds and the white citizens clamoring for the Indians' removal, he had no choice but to yield. Finally, on October 24, at Clark's St. Louis home, the prophet capitulated and signed away his followers' lands. In the Treaty of Castor Hill the Vermillion people surrendered their Vermillion River lands, while the Prairie Kickapoos of Missouri relinquished their holdings along the Osage.[29] It was the first time that Kenekuk had ever sold Indian lands. Perhaps the Great Spirit would consider the circumstances and cleanse Kenekuk's soul and not punish his people for violating the sacred command never to abandon the graves of their ancestors.

The Kickapoo Prophet had failed, for his people had to leave their cherished homeland. Despite all that Kenekuk had done to protect their rights, in the end it had proved of no avail. It mattered little that the Vermillion people were peaceful, sober, industrious, devout, and all the things the whites demanded that they be; they still had to move. Kenekuk's followers had adapted themselves to white society—they had acculturated—but had not assimilated. To the settlers, they were still different, for they had Indian ways and red skins, and whites refused to accept the Indians as equal members of the overall community. Their most unforgivable offense, however, was that they occupied fertile lands that white settlers coveted and were determined to have. Even the Great Spirit apparently lacked the power to stop this tragedy.

In the early autumn of 1832 about four hundred Vermillion

Indians packed their belongings and began the westward journey. By October they had reached the banks of the Mississippi in western Illinois, where they encamped for the winter a short distance from the home of the Indian agent Thomas Forsyth. When he heard that some Indian travelers had arrived, the curious agent went to greet them. "I found them to be the Prophet or Preachers party," Forsyth related; "in going to their camp I was much surprised to find their dogs so quiet and peaceable." He was favorably impressed by Indians who did not drink whiskey or paint themselves; they "never made, or intended to make, war against any people"; and they never steal, "tell lies or do anything bad." Kenekuk's religion had such a wonderful influence over the people, Forsyth concluded, "that it ought to be encouraged by the government as it inculcates peace and good will to all men." He had little doubt that Kenekuk would win new converts in the West, and he hoped that other tribes would flock to the religion that could well hasten the "civilization" of these unfortunate peoples.[30]

Kenekuk was troubled about his violation of the Great Spirit's commands, however, and he appealed again to William Clark to let his people remain in Illinois. Although Clark was sympathetic, the decision for removal was irrevocable, and in January 1833 he advised the prophet to continue the journey "as soon as possible to your new country. Try it, perhaps you may find it better than it has been represented." The superintendent had some extra provisions delivered to ensure that the women and children would be comfortable. To his "friend" Kenekuk, he also sent as gifts a horse and a winter coat, so that the prophet might travel in a style befitting a great leader.[31]

Perhaps in the West, in a land later to be called Kansas, the Vermillion Kickapoos and their friends would prosper;

Kenekuk was optimistic, despite the adversity. Their journey would by no means be a "trail of tears," for he had prepared and organized his followers well. In the spring of 1833 the brave and determined Vermillion band arrived in the new land, still believing that the Great Spirit would remain forever by their side. These "chosen people" would make a fresh beginning in Kansas.

6. Kenekuk's Village on the Missouri

During the early months of 1833, Kenekuk and about four hundred followers, including over a hundred Potawatomi converts, settled along the west bank of the Missouri River, a few miles north of Fort Leavenworth. They immediately constructed their traditional bark wickiups and fashioned tables, chairs, and beds out of rushes that grew along the river bottoms; that spring they planted fields of corn, beans, squash, and other crops. A short time later, a white visitor found their village situated in "a retired, rural spot, shut out from the world, and looked as if it might have been free from its cares also."[1] This idyllic description, however, was far from accurate during those early days in the new land.

About one mile upriver lived the Prairie Kickapoos, recent arrivals from Missouri who had also surrendered their lands in the 1832 Treaty of Castor Hill. Long standing differences between the two bands, aggravated by their new proximity, resulted in frequent bickering and strife. They quarreled constantly over moral, financial, and legal matters. While Kenekuk's men farmed and generally remained close to their village, the Prairie Kickapoos preferred more traditional ways; they shunned agriculture and white civilization. A traveler described the Prairie Kickapoos as "a forlorn-

looking set" with "swarthy features and dingy blankets con-
trasting strikingly enough" with civilized society. A
Presbyterian missionary observed that these Indians were
"opposed to religion, schools etc., get drunk and gamble,
[while] there are but few of the Prophet's band that engage
in these habbets or wickedness."[2]

Governmental officials, meanwhile, were not concerned
about the essential incompatibility of the two Kickapoo
bands. Their major concern was that the Kickapoos
acknowledge the "benevolent" nature of the removal policy
and not hold a grudge against the Jackson administration.
The optimistic commissioner of Indian Affairs, Elbert Herring, wanted the bands to "consider us friends and not
wrongdoers," for if content, "they would remain at peace,
cultivate the arts of social life and advance in civilization."[3]
Herring's attitude was typical of federal administrators who
held little regard for Indian customs and believed in the total
superiority of white culture. Presumably, now that the
Kickapoos were living in isolation west of the Mississippi,
they could, in some mysterious manner, learn the ways of
"civilization" with little difficulty. Such baseless assumptions
naturally proved overly optimistic.

By the spring of 1833, Kenekuk's followers seemed to be
happy with their new homes as they tended their crops and
participated in tribal religious ceremonies. Upriver, at the
Prairie Kickapoo village, however, signs of discontent were
evident as Chief Kishko complained that the land was "not
equal to his expectations."[4] The new territory, moreover, was
less than half the size of their former range in Missouri. To
make matters worse, the Prairie Kickapoos felt uncomfort-
able living so close to Kenekuk's pious followers.

When these complaints reached Washington, Commissioner Herring ordered the special governmental envoys

Henry Ellsworth, John Schermerhorn, and Montford Stokes to visit the Kickapoos, examine their lands, and make any reasonable adjustments to satisfy the bands. The three commissioners had been assigned by President Jackson to travel among the newly relocated tribes in present-day Oklahoma, Kansas, and Nebraska, and to make sure that the Indians were settled comfortably. Herring informed the agents that the Kickapoo situation must be handled delicately. It was very important, he wrote, "to convince [the Kickapoos] that their removal was urged upon them to promote their own welfare, and that, under the pledge of protection guarantied to them, by the Government, it acknowledges the duty, as it is their desire, to study the true interests of the different tribes, and to advance their prosperity and happiness by all proper and consistent means."[5]

On a late summer morning in 1833, Commissioner Henry Ellsworth, with his son Edward serving as secretary, left Fort Leavenworth on horseback to visit the Kickapoo villages; the other two commissioners were ill and unable to travel. Accompanying the Ellsworths on the four-mile ride was the aspiring writer John Treat Irving, a nephew of the popular novelist Washington Irving. Since his arrival in early August, the Kickapoos had fascinated Irving, who was anxious to see how they lived. He had often observed these "pretty hard customers" carrying furs and skins and "driving bargains" with the fort sutler. "There were many manly forms among them," he noted later, "and some of their females were even beautiful. Scarce a day elapsed that we did not catch a glimpse of the gaudily dressed figures of some band, their tin trinkets glistening in the sunbeams, and their bright garments fluttering in the wind, as they galloped over the prairie towards the garrison."[6]

For more than an hour the men rode leisurely through

forest and over prairie, crossing several streams until they reached the apex of a high bluff overlooking the two Kickapoo villages. The view was quite picturesque. "At our feet lay a small green prairie, dotted with clusters of wildflowers," Irving noted. Three sides of the prairie were enclosed by a ridge of hills, and the men could see a clear stream shaded by many large trees, as well as flowers of countless varieties ornamenting the abundant valley grass, and a dense woods bordering the Missouri River.[7]

As they ventured down toward the two villages, the white men took with them the typical nineteenth-century preconceptions about Indians. To Irving and the Ellsworths, tribal culture was inferior and Indians were lazy and shiftless. "The troops of naked children who followed at our heels," wrote Irving, "convinced us, that among the sundry and manifold cares of the world, this tribe had not forgotten to perpetuate their race, and not withstanding their laziness, had contrived to start a fresh growth of papooses, that constituted the 'rising generation,' and were then undergoing the education, usual to the Indian child." He had little doubt that these children would inherit the slothful ways of their parents.[8]

The parents, moreover, were themselves mere "children of the forest" who lacked Christian morals and values. Irving's description of Kickapoo life was, more than anything else, a reflection of his own prudish morality:

> Here and there, winding through the woods, or strolling over the prairie, might be seen a couple of cooing, greasy lovers; full of affection and slovenliness; unwashed but devoted. What a fund of affection there must have been to have overlooked such a world of defects. A loud cry broke out in one of the hovels, and a couple rushed out. The first was

a fat blowsy squaw. After her followed a diminutive, spider-legged Indian, who looked as if he had withered away under the gall of his own disposition. He was the lord and master of the lady. In his hand he flourished a stick, with which he had been maintaining that discipline, by some deemed proper in a family, and which he now seemed inclined to continue. The woman, however, escaped and made for the woods. The bystanders paused for a moment to look on, for there was an agreeable excitement about this, which did not occur every day, and which therefore was not to be lost. Upon the escape of his wife, the little man looked around, as if he longed for some other object, upon which to vent his anger and wrath; but finding none, he disconsolately entered his dwelling.[9]

A meeting with the Vermillion Kickapoo leaders Pashacheha, or Jumping Fish, and Kenekuk forced Irving to modify his opinions somewhat. "The former was a corpulent man," noted Irving, "and in his youth must have been peculiarly handsome." The sophisticated easterner was quite taken with the Kickapoo Prophet, who greeted Irving after setting aside a long rifle that he was carrying. Kenekuk's stately bearing and eloquent speech made a deep impression on the white man: "There is an energy of character about him which gives much weight to his words, and has created for him an influence greater than that of any Indian in the town. From the little we saw it was evident that the chief yielded to him, and listened to his remarks with the deference of one who acknowledged his superiority. There was however no appearance of jealousy or heart burning between them."[10]

On September 2, Commissioner Ellsworth convened a council to discuss the Prairie Band's dissatisfaction with the new lands. Ellsworth began by praising the location, pointing out that the Missouri River allowed the Indians easy access and transport for agricultural and other trade goods. Nearby Fort Leavenworth, moreover, protected the Kickapoos from their enemies; what more could they want? He ordered the contending bands to live together peacefully, for the government would never approve of a tribal separation. "Your great father considers the Kickapoos a brave nation, and wishes all the warriors together," he sanctimoniously announced. Stay on this land, he advised, "and your great father will make good all his promises. The Great Spirit knows what has been said is true."[11]

A discontented Prairie spokesman named Muscahtewishah countered that their new reservation was too close to white settlements. The young men suffered from the effects of the "wicked water" that traders brought over from Missouri, and the Indians wanted to move to a more isolated location on the Marais des Cygnes River to the southwest. He talked on, pointing out the differences between the Prairie Kickapoos and Kenekuk's followers. The prophet had exercised a confusing influence over the Indians; his preachings had caused tribal factionalism to flare up. "Our young men and the chiefs do not agree, as they did some time ago; some wish one thing, some another. Some wish to go to the Prairie, where there is game." Others wanted to remain and raise corn. "We are like fish, we jump at whatever is thrown. I cannot get settled in my own mind."[12]

Chief Kishko led those who wanted to relocate on the Marais des Cygnes, and he adamantly insisted that the Kickapoos be allowed to move.[13] He pointed out that many Prairie Kickapoos already lived south of the Kansas River on the Shawnee reserve, "occupied I think in drinking and rioting"; those Indians needed his leadership. At the present reservation on the Missouri, moreover, the women and children might freeze during the winter, or a cholera epidemic might break out. The government should resettle them all on new lands before it was too late.

Kenekuk's followers, in contrast, had few complaints. They realized that game was relatively scarce along the Missouri River, but it had been in Illinois as well. The present location possessed fertile soil, capable of producing abundant crops, and the band would depend largely on agriculture for subsistence. The rich pasture, moreover, could support large numbers of ponies and cattle, and there was enough wood for fuel and building purposes. For these reasons, Chief Jumping Fish turned to the Vermillion people and proclaimed: "I was the first to come and settle on these lands after the others had signed the treaty; I then thought that the minds of all had been settled. The land is good, and I like it."[14]

The council ended with the Prairie Band still dissatisfied. The next month, Ellsworth called the Kickapoos to Fort Leavenworth and told them that their present site was "most favorable"; and he warned Kishko and his followers to remain on their reservation. Kishko indignantly replied that he only wanted to hunt game along the Marais des Cygnes, not to stay there permanently; a short time later, however, the disgruntled chief and several of his followers left and eventually joined kinsmen who were living in Texas and Mexico. With them gone, the opposition leadership was temporarily weakened, and those who favored the present reserve were in the majority. Expressing the prevailing sentiment, Kenekuk and Jumping Fish declared that they were "willing to accept the land, and say no more about it." On November 8 the gratified Ellsworth relayed the news to officials in Washington "that the Kickapoo dissatisfaction with their land is removed . . . the land is good and water communication most easy. *The chiefs have accepted the land* and are now anxious to have the things [farming tools and a gristmill] promised in the treaty."[15]

Commissioner Ellsworth's assessment of the situation was far from accurate. When Kishko left, an Indian named Pashishi assumed the leadership of the remaining Prairie Kickapoos. "He is a savage in the full extent of that term," the Jesuit Peter Verheagen said of Pashishi a few years later; "He paints his face black, with a little red around the eyes, and he glorifies in the fact that he has adopted no single article of the white man's dress."[16] The chief and his Prairie Band followers were still angry that the officials had assigned them land that lacked sufficient timber and game, and they resented governmental interference in tribal affairs. Never enamored of white civilization, the Prairie people resisted governmental efforts to change their traditional ways, and they continually left the reserve to hunt and wander where they pleased. In April 1834, Agent Richard Cummins informed Superintendent Clark that the Indians remained dissatisfied and were still demanding to be relocated.[17]

Over the next few years, Cummins found Kenekuk's followers "well disposed" and easy to manage, but he had his hands full when it came to the Prairie Kickapoos. To his dismay, the Prairie tribesmen often squandered their treaty annuities on gambling and whiskey. Visiting the villages on May 21, 1835, the agent found the band in a "deplorably drunken condition." Making matters worse, Kenekuk's sober followers had difficulty protecting women and children from the drunken revelers. The men were prevented from working the fields for fear of having their wives and daughters molested in their absence. Cummins decided to stay around to make sure that the situation did not deteriorate further, but to his disappointment, the debauchery continued. "During the night I could hear them whooping in every direction," he related. In the morning he hurried off to Fort Leavenworth, seeking assistance.[18]

Cummins returned that afternoon, accompanied by a squad of troops. When they found and destroyed fifteen gallons of whiskey, the agent mistakenly believed that the crisis was over. "During the night if possible they were more noisy than they were the night before," he lamented. Determined to teach the transgressors a lesson, he returned again to the fort.

On May 23, Capt. Matthew Duncan, with forty-five well-armed cavalrymen, stormed into the Prairie Kickapoo village. Pandemonium ensued, as drunken Indians scattered into the nearby brush with the troops in hot pursuit. Soldiers combed the village but were unable to find any whiskey. They then grabbed one frightened Indian and threatened to throw him into jail if he refused to uncover the contraband. He quickly revealed the hiding place, whereupon the soldiers destroyed fifty gallons of liquor and made two arrests. Afterward, Captain Duncan reported regretfully that one of those in custody was the brother of Pashishi, "the principal chief, who had the magnanimity to inform on him."[19]

Although Duncan assured his superiors that "whiskey will not again be introduced to the same extent" among the Prairie Kickapoos, who would "now devote themselves to the cultivation of the small crops which they have on hand," the Indians continued their usual ways. Their behavior often shocked whites. When a steamboat docked near Fort Leavenworth, a passenger noted that the Prairie Kickapoos, who "instantly flooded" aboard, demanded and received tobacco and brandy. "They greeted the boss of the station affectionately," the traveler related, "wringing his hand and calling him 'papa, papa.' They played cards with great enthusiasm and even passion, and remained on board very late that night; and three young Indian women remained on board all night! . . . and with the consent of the chief of the tribe."[20]

The Kickapoo Prophet considered such behavior reprehensible, and he admonished Pashishi's people to "be wise and behave" and to stop "running after liquor." Kenekuk realized that their rowdy actions and drunkenness threatened tribal unity and made both bands vulnerable to attacks by aggressive whites intent once more upon taking the Kickapoos' lands and possessions. He threatened to invoke his supernatural powers to destroy Pashishi if the latter failed to reform; the prophet would "blow into a flame that would not be easily smothered, [and] perhaps cause his death."[21]

Pashishi paid little heed to Kenekuk's bluff, however, and when word of the Seminoles' triumph over American troops under Maj. Francis Dade in Florida reached the villages in the spring of 1836, the Prairie Band staged a boisterous "victory" dance that quickly got out of hand. Consuming several casks of whiskey, the celebrants began to rejoice that "the time was near at hand when the white people would all be subdued, and red men restored again to their country." When drunken Indians rode through Kenekuk's village, molesting women and destroying property, the prophet rushed to Fort Leavenworth, seeking aid from the soldiers.

Outraged by the Indians' celebration of an American defeat, the officials brought charges against Pashishi and his band. Calling the Indians together at the fort on June 13, 1836, Captain Duncan informed them that their behavior was an "insult" to the United States. After all the "favors" the federal government had done for the Kickapoos, Duncan scolded, they should "be grateful" and not hostile. "You have heard the charges against you," he shouted. "What have you got to say to them? Are these things true or are they false?"

Pashishi was in an unrepentant mood; he refused to admit to any wrongdoing. "I deny it all," he heatedly replied. "It is not true . . . we all deny that there is any truth in this account." Launching into a tirade against William Clark, Pashishi charged that the superintendent had deceived him by forcing his people to live close to the prophet's band.[22] "Our red-headed father at St. Louis [Clark] picked out this place for us to live on, and our chiefs moved with us here. But now we are here we find a great deal of contention between our chiefs." If Clark "had told me about the *bad wind* that is always blowing about the land at my village, he could never have persuaded me to move to it. He said that my father [Duncan] at this Garrison had very big eyes, and that he would see all my enemies, and defend me against them. But instead of this my father are watching me to see if I do anything wrong, . . . [and] he writes it down and sends it off to his General."[23]

Pashishi admitted that the celebration had been held, but he wondered why the officials made such "a great deal of fuss" over a simple religious ceremony. "It is the right of all people to dance," he pointed out, "the white as well as the red man dance. When we had this dance we did not expect any fuss about it." He demanded that the agents and soldiers stop interfering in Kickapoo affairs, and he resented efforts to stop the flow of whiskey to the villages. "It was the white people who first made whiskey and brought it among us," the chief insisted, "and as soon as we began to love it, you prohibited them and all others from bringing it among us."

When Pashishi had finished speaking, it was the Kickapoo Prophet's turn to vent his anger. But Kenekuk's displeasure was with the Prairie Band, not with the federal government.

I know one thing, that is, if all my chiefs and young men would . . . *be wise* and behave themselves, they would never hear of the *bad wind* that Pashishi talks about.

All I wish is that my people will *never again* interfere with bad things. If they *never had acted badly* they would not now [have] been called to this place. And I do wish that when we are again called here it may be for some good purpose. I look up to my great father for advice, and whatever he wishes me to do, I will try to do it, and what he wants my young men to do I want them to do it also. I will not change my mind and will always look up to my great father. I would be glad to see all these things settled. My chiefs have taken you [Duncan] by the hand and I hope all will be well in the future. You will let our great father know about his red children.[24]

The council ended with Kenekuk and Pashishi still bickering over the consequences of the dance. But the officials decided not to pursue the matter further. "That there was something wrong about the dance I have no doubt," Duncan wrote to Gen. Henry Atkinson, "but whether it was intended to celebrate the defeat of Major Dade and his party, I cannot pretend to say." It was widely known, he continued, that Kenekuk was a "religious enthusiast" who had frequently threatened to drive away the Prairie Kickapoos for refusing to adhere to his moral tenets. Because the Prairie Indians meant no harm to the white people, officials were content to forget the incident altogether.[25]

Kenekuk was determined to settle matters in his favor, and throughout the following years he held firm rein over his followers, admonishing them to live according to the Great Spirit's commands. His people refrained from carousing and riotous behavior, and they adhered to a Protestant-like work ethic. Because the government was slow to provide adequate farm equipment, they used primitive tools to plow their fields; they planted corn, beans, and other crops, and sold their surpluses at the fort. Although they insisted on their communal ways and refused to consider individual land ownership, many whites acknowledged that the Indians were making progress. The Baptist missionary Isaac McCoy believed that "the Prophet's influence has made them more industrious than they formerly were." The Methodist minister Nathaniel M. Talbott conceded that the Kickapoos "raise more corn and try harder to live than most of the tribes." A government-employed schoolteacher praised his young Kickapoo charges: "Their intellect is strong and lively, their memory quick and retentive, their morals good, their manners pleasant, and they are remarkably active and industrious." A trader counted Kenekuk's Potawatomi converts as "among the best Indians we have: industrious, sober, and most of them religious."[26]

Agent Cummins glowingly reported that the Vermillion Band almost equaled whites in government, farming, and religion. On January 31, 1838, he wrote Superintendent Clark that Kenekuk's people worked so hard that it was "astonishing" to observe the progress they had made since their arrival in Kansas. A few months later the agent told Clark that he had lived near Indians since he was a boy, "and I am sure I never knew any that made such proficiency in agricultural pursuits as the Kickapoos (Kennakuck's band) has in the last four years, and they evince a determination of perseverance, they are at this time truly in the spirit of work, if they continue to progress . . . the next four years as rapidly as they have the last they will be ahead of any Indians in this section of the country." That fall, Cummins informed Commissioner of Indian Affairs Carey A. Harris that Kenekuk's followers "attend closely to their church discipline, and very few ever indulge in the use of ardent spirits."[27]

While Kenekuk's followers were prospering, many Prairie Kickapoos continued to suffer from alcoholism. Cummins pointed out that white people, apparently "void of all conscience," traded whiskey to the Shawnees, Delawares, and Kickapoos. Unscrupulous border settlers plied the Indians with "ardent spirits" and then stole their horses, guns, and blankets. "Some freeze to death when drunk," the agent reported in October 1839, and "several drunken Indians have been drowned in the Missouri River this season, aiming to cross when drunk." He urged the passage of more stringent laws to suppress the many "dishonorable and dishonest" whiskey peddlers who "condescend to the meanest of acts."[28]

Pashishi admitted that his people needed to change their ways, and he regretted that they had failed to get along with Kenekuk's band. He agreed with the prophet that if "it was not for the difficulties growing out of drinking and stealing we could live together as brothers, and not be ashamed to look at one another."[29] The constant bickering between the two bands, however, eventually proved too much for the Prairie Indians, and by 1839 most of them had emigrated to Indian Territory, Texas, or Mexico. In that year, Pashishi and several Prairie Kickapoo families moved to a new location on the reservation, about twenty miles from Kenekuk's village.[30] With them gone, the Kickapoo Prophet held firm command and was free to continue the mission work that he had begun over twenty years earlier. But although he had outmaneuvered his Indian rivals, Kenekuk realized that even greater stumbling blocks lay in the path to true success for his people. Among these obstacles were the many missionaries who flocked to the Kickapoo village, hungry for converts to Christianity and to the ways of the white man.

7. Kenekuk
and the Missionaries

The arrival of Kenekuk and the Vermillion people in the West in 1833 immediately attracted the attention of Christian missionaries intent on winning Indian souls. At first, Kenekuk and his followers appeared to accept the priests and ministers with open arms. The Indians intended to reestablish their prosperous way of life along the western banks of the Missouri, and they knew that the missionaries could act as intermediaries between them and a federal government that was painfully slow in delivering promised treaty annuities.

Over the ensuing years, Catholics and various Protestant groups founded missions and schools on Kickapoo lands, confidently embarking on the task of converting Kenekuk's followers to Christ's ways while convincing them of the superiority of white culture. Firm believers in the American melting pot, the missionaries were certain that Christ's teachings and an appreciation for the "manual arts" would radically improve the Indians' way of life. But making Christians out of "heathens" remained the missionaries' primary goal, and the Kickapoo Prophet's religion so closely resembled Christianity that most preachers thought conversion would be easy.

Despite their initial optimism, the missionaries found, over

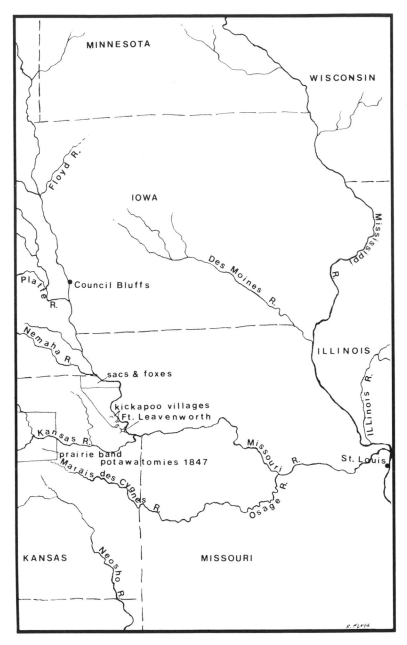

The Kickapoo village locations in Kansas, 1833–1854.

time, that they won but few disciples. While the Vermillion people willingly adapted to white society's secular ways, they paid scant attention to the Gospel. Their loyalty to Kenekuk's religion frustrated and angered the white clergy, who eventually left Kickapoo country to work among more credulous Indians.

The Baptists made the first attempt at proselytizing among the relocated Kickapoos and their Potawatomi allies. In May 1833, Isaac McCoy instructed the Reverend Daniel French to visit the Kickapoos, who reportedly had asked the Baptists to educate the Indian children. Because Kenekuk's people seemed devout, worked hard, and abstained from alcohol, Baptist expectations for success were high. Their hopes were quickly dashed, however, for the Indians stubbornly maintained a "remarkably uniform" attachment to the prophet. "For a few weeks it was hoped that the religious disposition of the party would facilitate our labours among this tribe generally," McCoy wrote, "but in this we soon discovered that we had been mistaken." After a short stay, French left because both the Vermillion and the Prairie bands had rejected his overtures. Later, the disgruntled McCoy admitted that Kenekuk's followers displayed a few good ethics, but the Baptist claimed that in actual practice "the morals of the party were scarcely, if any better, than those of their dissolute kindred." To McCoy, their religious beliefs were merely "a step from savage blindness into greater absurdity."[1]

The Kickapoos enjoyed only a brief respite before other preachers arrived to "save" them from their "heathen" ways. In July 1833, the Presbyterian missionary William Smith visited the villages and found the Indians "moral in their deportment and . . . very sincere in their religion"; he astutely concluded that Kenekuk's faith was too strong to counteract. Smith thought that the Jesuits might have better success, because the prophet's religion closely resembled Catholicism, and he quickly abandoned thoughts of establishing a Presbyterian station in the area.[2]

Shortly after Smith's departure, one of the most colorful characters ever to preach in Indian country appeared. Her name was Harriet Livermore, and she was determined to save the entire world, not just the Indians, from the clutches of Satan. As the daughter of a New Hampshire congressman, Livermore had enjoyed the excitement of Washington social life until a young man had rejected her affections. Withdrawing into a deep depression, she felt that her previous life had been meaningless: "Where were the hours I had sacrificed to the God of this world, in dancing, card playing, novel reading and foolish talking?" After a period of mourning, she decided to start anew: "It was in September, A.D. 1811, that tired of the vain, thoughtless life I had led, sick of the world, disappointed in all my hopes of sublunary bliss, I drew up a resolution in my mind to commence a religious life— to become a religious person."[3]

She renounced her old ways and became a disciple of the Philadelphia humanitarian Elias Boudinot, who suspected that the American Indians were one of the lost tribes of Israel. Boudinot was convinced that the millennium was imminent and that the Indians were God's chosen people. He died in 1821, but Livermore had found his ideas convincing and would eventually seek out the Indians for her own spiritual fulfillment.

In an age when professional women were rare, she became an itinerant preacher and by the late 1820s was famous (or notorious) in the eastern states for her spellbinding sermons. Writing to a friend in April 1827, Dolley Madison said of Livermore: "I for one would go to listen to her in search of light! But is she of the pure in spirit, filled with true religion without alloy, or does worldly ambition for éclat tarnish the perfection of the soul she possesses?" John Greenleaf Whittier called Livermore a "brilliant darkeyed woman, striking in her personal appearance and gifted in conversation"; his famous poem "Snowbound" featured this strange, "violent-tempered woman of indomitable will." John Quincy Adams detected "a permanency in this woman's monomania which seems accountable only from the impulse of vanity and the love of fame. The religious spirit easily allies itself to these passions, and they easily grasp the garb of religion."[4]

Livermore paid little attention to either public acclaim or ridicule. "As to being made a spectacle, a public show, a kind of by-word among a multitude, a derision and scorn to thousands, it does not affect me, when my heart is devoted to God."[5] Despite criticism from some quarters, she continued her crusade and in 1827 harangued a Washington audience that included President Adams and several congressmen, warning them to repent, for the end of the world was at hand. Five years later, after failing to persuade the citizens of Charleston, South Carolina, to free their slaves, she decided to take her message to the Indians.[6]

Livermore left Washington in May 1832, in search of the Indian prophet who preached rousing sermons on the true path to God's heart. Could this Indian be God's true messenger, the man who Boudinot had predicted would soon lead Indians—the chosen people—to the promised land? Although a "small voice" from above kept whispering " 'Thou must go to Jerusalem,' " Livermore's "face was then set as a flint towards the wilderness of America"; she had to find out for certain if this Indian was a bona-fide holy man.

For over a year she traveled slowly westward. "Other

females were in company with a husband, or a father, or a brother, or in charge of a Missionary, and a member of his family," she wrote with unconcealed pride; "I am conscientiously solitary!" She sallied forth, "undismayed by Cholera, sandbars, or floating timbers, by officers, soldiers, agents, traders, commissioners, or the devil."[7] In the summer of 1833 this Pilgrim Stranger, as she modestly called herself, finally arrived at Fort Leavenworth, where she expected "to pitch my tent with the prophet's band of the Kickapoo nation."[8]

Most of the details of her meeting with Kenekuk have been lost to history; but it seems likely that the Kickapoo Prophet politely greeted this woman who spoke directly to God and preached that Christ would soon return to save the red people from destruction. "Watch and pray," she warned, "for we know not at what moment the whirlwind may rise, and the horrible tempest come. The event of course is nigh— I believe at the doors; and the condition of my red brethren is one of the beacons that warns me. May God preserve us from falling into 'the great transgression!' "[9]

In August 1833, Livermore gave Kenekuk the dreadful news: Napoleon Bonaparte had risen from the dead as the Antichrist; Andrew Jackson's administration would be overthrown, and Napoleon's military dictatorship would impose its tyranny over the world. The rapture, she declared, was at hand! "It is the literal reign of anti-christ," the time when the devil will rule the world. "It is impossible to avoid this terrible object." She begged Kenekuk to give her sanctuary on Kickapoo lands, for on September 4 the Prophet Elijah would reappear to save the Indians from impending doom. The Hebrew prophet would swoop down to lift Kenekuk and all of the Kickapoos away from the chaos and transport them up to heaven.[10] Livermore had no intention of being left behind with Napoleon and the devil; she would cling to the skirts of Elijah and the Kickapoos as they made their flight to the promised land.

Kenekuk's reaction to Livermore's prophecy was not recorded, but the thought of spending an eternity with the Pilgrim Stranger was probably more than even a compassionate man could bear. He most likely listened politely, as was his nature, and then gave little more thought to this crazy white woman. Commissioner Henry Ellsworth's response, however, was clear and immediate. Astonished that William Clark had actually given Livermore permission to pursue her calling among the Indians, Ellsworth dashed off an urgent appeal to officials in Washington for the authorization to evict this "deranged" woman from Indian country. "It is true, her visit to the Kickapoos is by the consent of the Superintendent of Indian affairs at St. Louis," he wrote. "But I do not believe, Gen. Clark is acquainted with her present principles. With the kindest feelings as a Gentleman, to a Lady, I am decidedly of the opinion that her residence among the Indians can do no good and may do much harm."[11]

On August 18 the impatient Ellsworth took matters into his own hands; confronting Livermore, he demanded that she leave the area immediately. "The Government did not want to have the Indians believe that God communicated in an audible voice to their prophet," he told her. The recent Black Hawk War had demonstrated "the bad influence of Indian dreamers." The Indians, he insisted, needed to tend their crops and support their families; they had no time for "superstition." He promised to do what he "could as a gentleman to make her departure agreeable."[12]

But Livermore demurred, declaring that God had forbidden her from ever leaving, and she would go only if

shackled in irons. "My mind is pacified by the toil and morti-
fication I endure," she rhapsodized, "for a hope that my
testimony will be of some service to the Indians, and a determination to try to comfort them, stimulates my willing spirit
to persevere, and the weak, suffering flesh is forced to yield."
But when September 4 passed and Elijah failed to make his
appearance, she threw herself to the ground shouting: "What
shall I do?" Her mission had failed. "O! could I realize,"
she wrote, "that the murmuring breeze of the forests in
Missouri [Kansas], would mingle with my simple songs,
repeated by the Christian Kickapoo, or Potawattamie Indians, in their sorrowful days, my praises to God should as-
cend on the wings of the morning, on the cloud of the even-
ing, in strains of adoring gratitude, that he permitted me
to write them. But, alas! I fear this joy may never be mine.
Those tribes know not the white man's language."[13] The
Pilgrim Stranger soon departed on an even more quixotic
and heroic mission, for God had "ordered" her to Jerusalem
to spread Christ's teachings among the Jews.

Much to the relief of Ellsworth and the other federal officials, the dedicated souls who thereafter descended on the
Kickapoo villages preached more conventional doctrines. On
November 18, 1833, just ten days after Ellsworth had temporarily eased the Prairie Band's displeasure with the new
lands, the Jesuit Father Benedict Roux arrived to scout out
prospects for a Catholic mission. Roux especially hoped to
confer with the Kickapoo Prophet, but Kenekuk and most
of the other men were away hunting. The priest was not
discouraged, however, because women, children, and old
people flocked around him like "an angel sent from heaven."
He was pleased to find that they "pray every day, morning,
night and before meals; they sanctify Sunday as we do and
spend it entirely in prayer. They do not swear nor wage war,

nor lie, nor have more than one wife; they believe in Heaven, Purgatory and Hell, [and] honor the Blessed Virgin and Saints." The Jesuit wrote to his superiors in St. Louis that Kenekuk had "two very docile sons, who, like their father, show themselves favorably inclined towards religion." If God would only send one of them to the priesthood, he thought, "what mighty conquests for religion would then ensue!" Because of all the "edifying things" that he had witnessed, Roux was sure that a Catholic mission would be a tremendous success. His favorable report prompted Catholic officials to initiate plans for a station on the Kickapoo grounds.[4]

When Roux returned to the villages for a brief visit on January 1, 1834, Kenekuk told him that the Indians were anxious for the "blackrobes" to show them the way to heaven. The prophet had good reason for making a favorable impression on the priest. Kenekuk knew that the Indians' economic security would be enhanced if the federal government were to live up to its treaty commitment to provide money, farm tools, housing supplies, and educational needs. Because the Kickapoos' repeated pleas for promised federal assistance had fallen on deaf ears, he had decided to allow missionaries, who had greater influence over Washington bureaucrats, to proselytize among his people. Although he realized that the priests and ministers posed a threat to his authority, Kenekuk had enough confidence in his own religious powers to permit competition from outsiders.

Before the Catholics could act, the Methodist minister Jerome C. Berryman wandered into the villages with plans of his own. Sometime in January 1834, Berryman spent his first night in a Kickapoo wickiup and discovered that it would take hard work to "civilize" these "very strange" people. He noted the Indians' blankets, breechcloths, leggings, and buckskin moccasins as evidence of their primitive nature. Their bark wickiups, crude furnishings, and homemade farming tools, moreover, convinced him that these people "had never been, properly speaking, settled, but had always led a roving life."[15]

Berryman was, nevertheless, greatly pleased by the devoutness and the conduct of the prophet's followers. "When I went to that people," he recalled, "I found among them a man of their own tribe by the name of Ke-en-e-kuk who exercised unlimited sway over the larger portion of the tribe, but the rest [the Prairie Kickapoos] despised him. The last named, however, were opposed to any innovations upon their savage habits, and consequently opposed to missions and schools." The Methodist was encouraged when, after an initial coolness, Kenekuk invited Berryman to preach at Kickapoo services. Within a short time, the preacher had baptized over four hundred Indians, including the prophet himself. Berryman's superiors were so enthusiastic about their prospects for winning converts that they gave Kenekuk a Methodist preaching license; they also promised him an annual salary of two hundred dollars to serve as a preacher's assistant.[16]

Convinced that the prophet had been a practicing Christian for about twelve years, Berryman asserted that Isaac McCoy had made a "great mistake" in implying that the Indian leader knew little theology. The more perceptive Methodist reckoned that the Kickapoos and their allies had been without proper guidance for so long that "their theory and practice of religion would be imperfect." Although Kenekuk's followers had "many religious peculiarities foreign to Christianity," they were "truly pious" and "united with us." Kenekuk further convinced the preacher about his sincerity when he advised his followers to seek out Berryman for religious instruction. The white minister was happy to comply; within a few months he and his wife, Sarah, were teaching about forty children in a log schoolhouse that was built near the villages.[17]

Such efforts to convert Kenekuk's people as well as the Prairie Kickapoos continued throughout those early years on the Missouri River. Most missionaries thought that the prophet's religion was a midpoint between paganism and Christianity, and they reasoned that with just a bit more education, his people would accept conversion. They found Kenekuk's capriciousness a hindrance at times, but they were sure that they could readily overcome this and other obstacles.

A few preachers, however, suspected that the prophet's religion would be difficult to counteract. Visiting the Berrymans on June 27, 1834, the Presbyterian missionary John Dunbar noticed that Kenekuk held "an almost unbounded influence" over his band. "Whatever the prophet says is law and gospel with them," Dunbar noted in his journal. He was impressed that the Kickapoo leader forbade stealing, lying, profane language, and whiskey drinking. "But whether he prohibits every vicious practice," Dunbar continued, "is quite doubtful. His religion may, perhaps, be said to be good, so far as it goes, but how far it does go precisely, I have not been able to ascertain."[18]

Dunbar returned in July with his colleague Samuel Allis, who had been anxious to learn about the prophet's religion. Allis was astonished by what he saw, especially the practice of flagellation. He later wrote, with more feeling than grammatical skill:

The Kikapoos and Potawatomies that were with them, have about nine correcters, which do all the whipping. These men

have small whittled stick they carry with 'em, attend the
metings to regulate the children and dogs, and see if all are
in there places, they also attend school, one or more of them,
to regulate the children, and if they are not there the teacher
must not whip the children, even parents are not permitted
to whip there own children. I believe Friday in each week is
whipping day with them, all that have done 'rong dureing
the week, come forward and confess and take a whipping,
this is sort of Catholic form. They also put a cross at the
graves of some of the dead.

The prophet says the Great Father (God), took him out
of his hart and placed him in this world. He went astray until about nine years since, reformed, and began to serve God,
and had since ben Holy; [he] has ben led by the Great Spirret to do good and lead his people (many of them) in the
right way. I am afraid his hart has not ben changed, but [he]
is a desineing man, and is imposing upon his people. I believe
to this is the opinion of Brother Berryman.

Some of his people, I believe, do as well as they know how;
they talk much about the good way and the bad way, and
about praying to the Great Spirret. [They] meet together often
to worship, and have a great many ceremonies, but they seem
to know little about Jesus Christ, and the way of salvation
thrue a Redeemer.[19]

Despite observations by astute outsiders that the Methodist
venture was doomed to failure, Berryman and his colleagues
remained ever hopeful. On January 28, 1835, after a year's
labor among Kenekuk's people, Berryman assured his
superiors that the "prospect of success, I have no hesitation
in saying, is good." A short time later, however, he complained that Kenekuk rarely allowed him to hold services in
the church that the government had recently built on the
reserve. Although the prophet insisted that his people were
too ignorant to understand the white man's words and kept

promising to ease them into Methodism, Berryman was dubious.

The Methodist preacher came to realize, moreover, that Kenekuk's "peculiar" methods always prevailed, and like Dunbar and Allis, Berryman was shocked that the Indians willingly submitted to corporal punishment. "I have often seen both men and women at their public meetings for worship come forward and receive a number of lashes on their bare backs, so well laid on as to cause the blood to run freely," he wrote later. "Many of them bore visible scars on their backs, caused by former flagellations. We found out finally that this presumptuous man [Kenekuk] claimed to be the son of God come again in the flesh, and that the Father had sent him to the red people this time as he did to the white people before!" This was superstitious nonsense, Berryman railed; he lamented the fact that many Indians believed that the shedding of blood was "expiatory in its effects, hence their willing submission to the lash."[20]

In spite of such misgivings, the Methodist superintendent Thomas Johnson remained optimistic. Although Johnson admitted in June 1835 that the Kickapoo mission had encountered some difficulties, these were "fast giving way, and I think our prospects of ultimate success are as good as they ever have been."[21] This was an accurate assessment—the Methodists' prospects had never been good. Their hopes were dealt a severe blow the following month, when another Jesuit priest arrived at the Kickapoo villages in response to Father Roux's encouraging reports to the Catholic authorities.

Father Charles F. Van Quickenborne was little concerned that the Methodists had already established a mission and school for the Kickapoo bands. In their relations with Indians, the Jesuits had always held several advantages over their Protestant counterparts. The blackrobes were not hindered by family responsibilities or financial concerns, and their vow of chastity was appreciated by the Indians, who realized that interracial unions often ruptured the tribes' political harmony. The priests' classical education, moreover, gave them a far greater understanding of other cultures. The blackrobes willingly made concessions to local customs, moreover, and unlike most Protestant ministers, they began serious mission work only after they had mastered tribal languages and had come to understand the folkways. The Jesuits had few qualms about debating theological questions with tribal religious leaders: they seized the opportunity to discredit competitors and to enhance Jesuit prestige among the Indians. Rather than attempting to stamp out traditional dances, games, and festivals, the blackrobes tolerated these native ceremonies and sought to merge them with Catholic rituals and permitted the Indians to express Catholic doctrine in their tribal language and thought structure.[22]

With this history of Jesuit success, Van Quickenborne had no inkling that serious difficulties might ensue when he began to proselytize among the Kickapoos. Father Roux's glowing reports had mentioned nothing about the Vermillion Band's well-established religion, which shielded the Indians against any outsider who might seek to change their ways. The ethnocentric Van Quickenborne would never admit that Kenekuk's moral code approximated that of the Jesuits, and he would scoff at Indian claims that they had already discovered the true path to salvation.

On July 4, 1835, the blackrobe ventured into the Kickapoo villages, determined to snatch Indian souls from the clutches of Satan as well as the Methodists. The following day was Sunday, and he was invited to say Mass at the home of Lawrence Pensineau, a trader for the American Fur Company. After Mass, the Kickapoo Prophet greeted the priest, and after a brief exchange of pleasantries, the two launched into a discussion of theology. Curious about the Jesuit's intentions, Kenekuk asked him to explain Catholic doctrine.

With a scornful air, Van Quickenborne seized this opportunity to demonstrate his superiority over an uneducated Indian. "We teach," he replied, "that every man must believe in God, hope in God, love God above all things and his neighbor as himself; those who do this will go to heaven, and those who do not will go to hell." The priest added that the biblical prophets had "proved through miracles that God had spoken to them."[23] This was an obvious attempt to discredit Kenekuk's claims that he was acting under the direct command of the Great Spirit.

The Kickapoo Prophet interrupted to proclaim that he too had performed miracles. "This is the very way I got to be believed when I began to preach," Kenekuk said; "I raised the dead to life. There was a woman, who, so everyone thought, could not possibly recover her health; I breathed on her and from that moment she began to improve and is now in good health. Another time I saw an infant just about to die; I took it in my arms and at the end of a few days it was cured."[24]

When Van Quickenborne blandly replied that Kenekuk had merely doctored the sick and had not performed any miracles, the Indian flared up in anger. A stranger had dared contradict the Kickapoo Prophet! After a few minutes, however, his vexation eased, for he recognized the futility of arguing with this contentious Jesuit. Kenekuk knew that with both Catholics and Methodists stationed among his people, the missionaries would have to compete for the Indians' favor, so he decided on a diplomatic approach. "I realize that my religion is not a good one," he admitted, "if my people wish to embrace yours, I will do as they say."

On the following Sunday, Kenekuk announced that the Great Spirit had long promised to send someone to help them complete their religious instruction. Perhaps the blackrobes were the answer to the Kickapoos' prayers; if his followers wanted to become Catholics, the prophet would allow it.

Van Quickenborne was skeptical about Kenekuk's motives: "God alone knows whether he spoke sincerely." Van Quickenborne was, however, less suspicious about the Prairie Kickapoos, when, after a council, Pashishi requested that "a blackrobe come and reside among us with a view to instruct us."[25]

With this invitation in hand, Van Quickenborne hurried to Washington to seek federal aid for a Catholic mission to the Kickapoos. Arriving in September, he established temporary headquarters at the Jesuit-operated Georgetown University, a short carriage ride from most federal offices. On September 17 he sent to federal authorities an outline of his plans for a mission. The Kickapoo chiefs, he avowed, "including even the prophet Kennekuk," had expressed their strong desire to have the Jesuits settle among them. "The prophet said that he had always hoped that a Black-gown . . . would be sent by the Great Spirit to help him in instructing his people and teaching them the truths he did not know." Five days later, Commissioner of Indian Affairs Herring agreed to provide the Jesuits with $500 to be paid as soon as they had built their school.[26] The commissioner realized that tensions were mounting between the Vermillion and Prairie Kickapoo bands, and he evidently thought that the Catholics could help to settle their quarrels.

On June 1, 1836, Father Van Quickenborne and three assistants disembarked from a steamboat near the Kickapoo villages and were immediately greeted by Kenekuk and Pashishi, as well as several other Indians. Van Quickenborne was confident that the Jesuits would win many souls, especially among the Prairie Kickapoos. He informed his superiors that Pashishi was "quite proud of the circumstance of our coming at his particular invitation and for this reason wished me to build near his town; on the other hand the Prophet expressed a wish that we should do as much for his band as for the others." To avoid hard feelings, Van Quickenborne decided to locate the station halfway between the rival villages.[27]

A few weeks later, Father Christian Hoecken arrived and immediately began to study the Kickapoo vocabulary. Because Hoecken mastered their language quickly, many Indians grew fond of him; they called the kindly priest their Kickapoo Father. He encouraged them to perform their own music at church services, and during Mass the Indians always "behaved modestly." But although Hoecken made friends easily, he found the winning of Indian souls more difficult; by the end of the year the Jesuits had converted two Kickapoo children, but no adults had consented to become Catholics. Father Peter Verhaegen, the superintendent of the Missouri Catholic Missionary Society, grimly noted during a visit to the mission that the Indians remained strongly "adverse to a change of their superstitious practices and vicious manners." Even the ever-optimistic Van Quickenborne grudgingly admitted that it was "one thing to come to the Indian mission and another to convert the Indians."[28]

Although many Indians pointed out that the Methodist school already more than served their needs, the Jesuit institution opened its doors early in 1837. The enrollment at Berryman's school had dropped from ninety to sixteen students since its inception three years earlier. While few children attended the Protestant school, fewer still went to the Catholic one. Those who did attend, furthermore, were usually more interested in food or presents than in reading, writing, arithmetic, and the catechism. In his 1837 school report, Father Verhaegan warned federal officials that if conditions did not improve soon, the Jesuits "might be compelled to abandon the buildings and the land (about 15 acres well fenced in), which would cost a loss to the society of at least $3000."[29]

The Jesuit endeavors had faced severe handicaps since the priests' arrival the previous year. Kenekuk, angry that the blackrobes called him a false prophet and denounced his religion, commanded his followers to ignore the Jesuits. Even Pashishi, who had invited the priests to build a mission, had become somewhat disenchanted. He nevertheless favored the Catholics over the Methodists; the most likely candidates for sainthood, he thought, were the priests. "It is very seldom that white people go to heaven," he reasoned. "If any get there it must be the preachers, particularly the blackrobes who keep no women at all." But he warned that if a priest ever tried "to change the old customs of my forefathers, I will *quiet him* and listen to him no more."[30]

When the Jesuits pressured the Prairie Kickapoos to attend Mass, settle down, and abstain from whiskey and gambling, the Indians responded in typical fashion. "We want no prayer," they announced; "our forefathers got along very well without it and we are not going to feel its loss." Despite such obstinacy, the priests' spirits remained high. "It is a well known fact that the Indians in general are predisposed in favor of Catholic Black-robes," Van Quickenborne wrote his superiors in February 1837. "With the help of God and with patience we can go far."[31]

But Van Quickenborne and his fellow missionaries never got far with the Kickapoos. By the summer of 1837, Van Quickenborne had exhausted his strength in endeavoring to make Christians out of them. On August 17 the seemingly indefatigable priest died following a brief illness; he was only fifty years old.

The other Jesuits tried to carry on, but their task proved impossible. By autumn, many Prairie Kickapoos had wearied of Jesuit attempts to change their ways. These Indians also resented Kenekuk's interference in their affairs and prepared to leave for more hospitable surroundings. Pashishi told Father Hoecken that whiskey peddlers from Missouri had also contributed to their discontent; alcoholism had affected his people so greatly that they must move or be destroyed. Drunken Indians, moreover, made poor farmers and even worse churchgoers.

Father Verhaegen was especially upset by the Jesuits' lack of success; he held Berryman and the Methodists primarily responsible. The Jesuits' failures, Verhaegen speculated, were owing "first to the presence and opposition of a Methodist Minister who lives among them, to the vicinity of the whites, and to the difficulties which always attend the commencement of such establishments." Thinking as much about the financial cost to the Church as about the loss of converts, Verhaegen wondered: "If the Kickapoos go away, what will become of the buildings which we have erected and the improvements which we have made?" He advised federal officials that in the future, priests must use primitive dwellings and build permanent structures only after they had become sure of reaping an ample harvest of Indian souls.[32]

When the disgruntled Prairie Kickapoos promised to return to their village after their winter hunt of 1837/38, Jesuit uneasiness subsided temporarily. But the Indians continued to reject the Jesuits' advances. Many Prairie Kickapoos, furthermore, never returned from their hunt, preferring to join kinsmen who were already living in Texas and Mexico. When the priests threatened to close the mission in the spring of 1838, Pashishi begged them to stay for at least another year; his people would surely have reformed by then. "It is I who invited you to come here," he pleaded. "I send my children to your school. You have done more good here in a year than others have done in five or six. You have cured our children of smallpox, you have befriended us in our needs, and you have been kind even to the wicked. The storm which makes the thunder roar above your heads will not last forever."[33]

The Jesuits' morale improved somewhat on May 21, 1838, when Father Pierre Jean De Smet arrived at the mission. Four days later the noted Jesuit had a long talk with Pashishi, who readily acknowledged that Catholicism was the true religion. The Prairie leader confided that he often had a "vision," or dream, of Jesuits in heaven, admonishing the Indians for their "unfaithfulness and vices." Because the Kickapoos had rejected the laws of Christ, Pashishi continued, "the Great Spirit had abandoned them to all sorts of irregularities and to the impositions of a false prophet [Kenekuk]." Failing to realize that these visions were similar to those of the Kickapoo Prophet, De Smet determined that Pashishi was "a man of good wit and good sense, who needs only a little courage to become an excellent Christian." De Smet advised his fellow priests to continue their labors, for surely they could overcome the "impositions" of one uneducated Indian—Kenekuk—and make the Catholic mission a success. After all, Catholicism was the one true religion; Kenekuk's faith was "heresy."[34]

Overcoming such heresy, however, proved impossible, because most of the remaining Prairie Kickapoos soon abandoned the reservation for locations far removed from the meddling missionaries. With the Prairie Indians gone, Kenekuk reigned supreme, and at Protestant-style frontier revivals he expounded his religious doctrines. He won adherents among other tribes in the region; since their days in the Wabash region, many Potawatomis had embraced the prophet's message of peace and love. The Potawatomis intermarried with the Vermillion Kickapoos, who gladly accepted the former as members of the band. Together they pledged their faith and devotion to Kenekuk.

Because most Kickapoos and Potawatomis felt a deep loyalty to Kenekuk, missionary efforts to win converts proved more difficult than ever, and by autumn 1839, attendance at the Catholic and Methodist schools was light. Jerome Berryman held that the "detrimental influence" of Kenekuk was responsible for keeping Indian children away from the Methodist classroom; it was nearly impossible to teach when students could "abscond and go home with impunity." The frustrated preacher blamed parental "ignorance and prejudice, instability and apathy," as well as the inherent laziness of the older students, for the breakdown in school discipline. He also lamented that the tribes avoided "true" men of the cloth, such as himself, and flocked to an "impostor" such as Kenekuk.[35] "The pretensions of these savage politicians are supported in the main by appeals to the credulity of the ignorant masses," Berryman intoned; such impostors were responsible for many evils in the world.

The pretenders have performed some wonderful deed, seen some dazzling vision, or received some startling revelation from the Great Spirit, all of which is received upon the bare assertion of the deceiver with a willingness proportionate to his audacity and the stupidity of his dupes. This is the way that the great leaders among savages rise to place and power. There may be now and then an honorable exception. It is the fruitful source of the miseries that have fallen upon the savage tribes of America, and would to God it were true alone of these.

Does not the heathen world groan beneath the accumulating evils which arise from ignorance, superstition and vice on the part of the many and the shrewdness, ambition, and presumptuousness of the comparatively few on the other hand? Every age has produced in every country minds of lofty aspirations, and nothing but intelligence and virtue can prevent the reckless and ruinous adventures of such minds. This class of men must be held in check by the counteracting influence of popular virtue, or they will in time barbarize the world. Our own distracted country is cursed with too many Ke-en-e-kuks today.[36]

Agent Richard Cummins blamed poor school attendance and the rejection of missionaries, not on the Kickapoo Prophet, but on the unfortunate death of the government-employed blacksmith. For some reason Cummins omitted details about this event in his reports to federal officials. It appeared, however, that the Kickapoos disliked their blacksmith and had been bickering with him for over a year. Sometime in 1839 he was killed, probably during an argument. The agent alleged that one of Kenekuk's sons was the culprit. While no charges were ever filed, Cummins noted that "after this unfortunate circumstance happened, there seemed to be a backwardness in some of the parents of the children in sending or letting them remain at school."[37] The Indians' general distrust of whites was probably strengthened by the incident.

In the years that followed, the Kickapoos and their Potawatomi allies generally shunned the missionaries. By 1840 the Jesuits and the Methodists were spending most of their time preaching to white settlers across the river in Missouri or to soldiers at Fort Leavenworth. The preachers resented Kenekuk and held him primarily responsible for their failure to win converts. Father Nicholas Point, who visited the Jesuit mission in late December 1840, was shocked by what he observed: "Here had our missionaries been laboring for five years in their midst, and yet on Sunday during Mass you could scarcely see more than one of them in attendance at the chapel." Point also condemned the Kickapoo Prophet: "By his cool effrontery and persevering industry, this man, who is a genius in his way, succeeded in forming a congregation of three hundred souls, whom he used to assemble in a church which the United States Government had built for him, and palsied all the exertions of four missionaries of the Society." When the Catholic station closed its doors for good on May 1, 1841, Point wept for the "mission which had been plunged into the deepest abyss of moral degradation by the scandalous conduct of a people who pretend to civilization."[38]

Kenekuk was a "false prophet!" railed the deeply resentful Father De Smet, who was appalled by the inexplicable failure of the Jesuit mission. "He calls himself the envoy of God, Christ under a new form, and invites all the nations of the earth to come and gather under his banner." The priest had trouble in rationalizing the fact that one illiterate "savage" had prevented the highly educated Jesuits from converting the unschooled "heathens." Like his fellow blackrobes, De Smet scorned those who regarded Kenekuk as their savior and was blind to the fact that the Indians' syncretic religion served their needs far better than did Catholicism. Caring little that the Vermillion people were sober, industrious, and moral, he denounced them for their stubborn unyielding faith in a pagan dogma. For want of a better reason, he decided that the prophet was "profoundly ignorant of Christian doctrines" and that Kenekuk's fol-

lowers were as "densely ignorant" of sin, confession, and
penance as the "rudest savages."[39] The Jesuits had little
choice, he conceded, but to leave Kickapoo country and reap
souls among less obstinate Indians.

The Methodists fared little better than the Catholics.
Jerome Berryman left in October 1841 to direct the Shawnee
Methodist Mission in present-day Johnson County, Kansas.
His successor, Nathaniel Talbott, found that he had little
to do, for only the few remaining Prairie Kickapoos bothered
to seek his spiritual advice. In May 1843 the visiting minister
William Patton noted that, although Talbott's preachings
were fairly well attended by the Prairie Kickapoos, most of
the Indians "did not seem to be much concerned about their
future and eternal interests. They appeared to be more anxious to have their faces well painted, and their persons
adorned after the manner of Indians, than to know what
they were to do in order to be saved; yet several of them gave
good attention, for awhile, to the things which were spoken."[40]

Although Talbott proselytized for several years, he won
few converts among the Kickapoos and Potawatomis. He
naturally blamed his meager harvest of souls on the "heathen
prophet" Kenekuk. Talbott informed his superiors that the
Indians "have among them a prophet who deceives them and
does all he can against the gospel." The Reverend Patton
confirmed that "Jesus Christ has no part in the religion
of the prophet. Let the church awake to their duty, and in
every responsible way labor to dispel these dark clouds of
superstition, sin and delusion."[41]

It was Methodism that was dispelled, however, and not
the prophet's religion. In the summer of 1848 the Reverend
Edmund Wright happened upon Kenekuk as the Indian
leader was visiting Weston, Missouri, just across the river

from the Kickapoo village. Wright noted that this was the same man who for many years "has had a separate congregation every Sabbath, and has opposed the [Methodist] mission, pretending to be the Indians' Savior and deriving his authority from certain characters on a 'chip' which he has called his Bible. Kenekuk has persuaded scores of Indians to believe that white men killed Jesus Christ before he had made an atonement for the Indians, and that he, Kenekuk, has been appointed by the Great Spirit to supply the deficiency."[42]

Kenekuk, ignoring the complaints of frustrated ministers and priests, carried on the work of the Great Spirit despite their hostility. The Kickapoo Prophet had outmaneuvered the white preachers, thereby ensuring a separate religious and cultural identity for his people. His next task was to provide for his followers' economic security while preparing them for the thousands of white settlers who would someday invade their lands. Throughout the 1840s his band prospered, unhindered by meddling preachers, and, unified by the prophet's religion, looked confidently to the future.

8. A Successful Future Assured

After the closing of the missions, Kenekuk's Vermillion Kickapoos endeavored to ensure a prosperous future for themselves with little help from the preachers or even from the federal government. They realized that white settlers would soon invade the Indian lands and pressure the Kickapoos to move again, so they pursued the ongoing revitalization of their tribal ways with renewed vigor. During the 1840s and early 1850s they formally adopted many long-time Potawatomi allies into the band, and the two groups lived together peacefully and without rancor. The numerous Potawatomi converts to Kenekuk's faith helped to strengthen the band during those critical years before the American Civil War.

Although the Vermillion Kickapoos and the Potawatomis had to make many difficult decisions and compromises as they adapted to changing conditions, they persevered by obeying the Great Spirit's commands and by following Kenekuk's strictures. Almost all of the other Indians who had been removed from the East eventually forfeited their Kansas lands to white settlers, but the Vermillion people survived; they may have surrendered their Illinois homes, but they never left Kansas. Even after Kenekuk's death, when their outlook for the future seemed bleak, the Vermillion Kickapoos and Potawatomis never forgot their ultimate goal; they worked "so that we may all, red and white, live together in peace and love."[1]

During the 1840s the Kickapoo Prophet devoted himself to strengthening his followers' defenses against the inevitable white assault on their lands and customs. Under his guidance Kickapoo and Potawatomi men worked hard to clear and plow the fields, and their farms provided their families with a secure living. Agent Cummins noted in his annual reports that these "lively, fearless, independent persevering people" had raised substantial surpluses of corn, beans, pumpkins, potatoes, beef, and pork, which they sold to traders for a profit.[2]

The success of these Indians was remarkable, considering the federal government's failure to abide by the financial provisions of the 1832 removal treaty. In July 1841, Cummins reported that many Indians were suffering "great anxiety" because the government had not sent any of the promised money, agricultural implements, or oxen. "Many families depend on the same team to break up the ground in the spring," he noted, which made some of them "very late" in planting their corn and other crops. Additionally, their gristmill needed repair and the dam had sprung a leak. Immediate help was needed, Cummins insisted. But the next year, the agent was still urging his superiors to loosen governmental purse strings, and he warned that his charges were losing patience: "Indians are always dissatisfied when they receive no answer, . . . [please] write something or they will place the blame on me and say that I neglected to write for them."[3]

On June 22, 1843, Kenekuk, Mecina, and Pashishi demanded that federal officials release the promised annuities: "We have always understood from our agent that our great father wanted his red children to lay aside their guns and go to work and live like his white children. This we want to do, but how can we work unless we have something to work with?"

A short time later, after the Methodist missionary Nathaniel Talbott had warned that Kenekuk was using the government's "seeming neglect to further his own purposes," federal assistance finally arrived. The funds helped to solidify the Vermillion Band's hold on its lands. By mid decade Thomas Harvey, the superintendent of Indian Affairs in St. Louis, reported that the Kickapoos, "a thrifty people" who "understand well the value of money," were prosperous and happy.[4]

The thriving condition of the Vermillion people brought other bands into the prophet's fold. When the Kickapoos had first settled along the Missouri River in 1833, they had been accompanied by many Potawatomi converts. In the years that followed more Potawatomis moved to the Kickapoo village. Many of them had formerly lived in Indiana, and some had emigrated from the Prairie Potawatomi reservation near Council Bluffs, Iowa. The industrious, sober, and pious newcomers gradually intermarried with the Kickapoos, and together they built houses and worked their farms; the Potawatomis also abstained from alcohol, gambling, and the other forbidden practices. In March 1844, Kenekuk and the other Kickapoo chiefs informed Agent Cummins that the two bands were so compatible that they had agreed to unite and form one "nation."[5]

When increasing numbers of Potawatomis settled on Kickapoo lands, however, federal officials demanded that they return to their own people. But the Indians refused to comply, insisting that the more traditional Prairie Potawatomis in Iowa might not survive the inevitable onslaught of white settlers onto their lands; the newcomers preferred to cast their lot with the Kickapoos. With Kenekuk's blessing they requested official authorization to merge with the Vermillion Band. "We have removed from Council Bluffs to Kickapoo Village," they informed Superintendent Harvey, "on account of the desolate habits of our chiefs and head men, in not listing to the wishes of our Great Father the President of the United States, in wishing them to cultivate the soil, and raise stock for their own use."[6]

Federal officials were forced to admit that these Potawatomis seemed to be better off than their Iowa brethren. Harvey noted in June 1844 that the Potawatomis abstained from whiskey and diligently tended to their crops and other responsibilities. The superintendent observed, however, that very few of them were sending their children to the Methodist school, and he held Kenekuk responsible for this deplorable state of affairs. On June 8 he wrote Commissioner of Indian Affairs Thomas Hartley Crawford that the bands "have among them one who is called the prophet (Kenekuck) who teaches some absurd notions: I understand his doctrines are rather moral, but his practices are not in accordance with his theory."[7]

For the next few years, federal officials ignored the fact that the Potawatomis had violated governmental regulations that required them to live on their assigned tribal lands. In the late 1840s, however, the authorities increased pressure on the émigrés to return to their own tribe, which had recently removed to a location on the Kansas River. For no apparent reason other than governmental expediency, officials in Washington demanded that all Potawatomis settle on one reservation, and in the autumn of 1848, the bureaucrats cut off annuity payments to those who refused to comply. When Indian agents ordered the Potawatomis to leave the Kickapoo village, they steadfastly refused, vowing to stay, whether or not the government paid them annuities. The officials should have known by then that the adherents of the Kickapoo Prophet were not easily intimidated.

Late in the following year the Potawatomis again asked permission to ally themselves legally with the Kickapoos. Under the leadership of the Potawatomi Chief Nozhakem, a devout follower of Kenekuk, they presented a formal petition to the commissioner of Indian Affairs on December 22, 1849: "We have for a number of years resided with our brothers the Kickapoos, and [we] have formed strong attachments for each other so that we can not now part. We think that it can make no difference to our Father so long as the Kickapoos are willing and anxious for us to remain with them." The local trader Samuel Mason agreed that they should be allowed to stay. The hard-working Potawatomis did not "want to go out on the Kansas river where their land lies," he wrote, "and they say they can't live with the Indians on [the] Kansas [who] . . . are lazy and drunken."[8]

Throughout 1850 and into 1851, Kenekuk worked to gain governmental approval for uniting the Kickapoo and Potawatomi bands. He realized that together they would be better able to resist the white settlers, who were again complicating matters for the tribes. The Vermillion Band was already complaining about the numerous white trespassers who stole property and assaulted members of the tribe. Settlements had sprung up across the river in Missouri, and whiskey peddlers, travelers, and thieves were frequenting Kickapoo country. On December 8, 1850, Kenekuk and Mecina beseeched federal authorities to stop a group of white men from cutting the valuable timber on the reservation. The audacious whites had erected several buildings and a steam sawmill and were cutting down trees without permission. Because much of the reservation was prairie, the prophet asked the St. Louis superintendent, David D. Mitchell, to take immediate action; the loss of timber and other resources was threatening the Indians' economic security.[9]

In the face of increasing outside pressure, the prophet worked to shore up his band's defenses, and he gave first priority to the union between the Kickapoos and the Potawatomis. On February 8, 1851, Kenekuk and Mecina met with a Missouri justice of the peace, John Collier, and signed a formal petition to legalize the Kickapoo-Potawatomi alliance. The chiefs maintained that the two bands had lived together for so many years that separation now would cause considerable grief and hardship. Kenekuk and Mecina argued that the Potawatomi émigrés had little in common with their cousins living along the Kansas River. Indeed, the adopted band had turned aside traditional ways and had taken Kenekuk's path to success and salvation. "Their religious principles," the chiefs continued, "which [are] taught by the prophet Kinecock [sic], they hold sacred."[10]

On that same day the Potawatomis also asked permission to remain. Over the past several years, Nozhakem and his people had "imbibed the religious tenets of the Kickapoo Prophet," they reminded federal officials; "their manners and habits have undergone an almost entire change since their residence among the Kickapoos." White friends of the Potawatomis corroborated this testimony. Charles A. Perry, a merchant who had known these Potawatomis for many years, agreed that they were far "more civilized and religious" than their Kansas River brethren. He told the officials that the former were determined to remain with Kenekuk's people, with or without the government's blessing.[11]

Finally, on May 9, 1851, Superintendent Mitchell relented and allowed the two groups to merge. Under Kenekuk's leadership they would henceforth constitute one band, in which all individuals had equal rights, and would share everything as brothers and sisters. "The terms of this national agreement make them one nation for all future time," Mitchell informed Commissioner Luke Lea. "Both parties were much pleased with the arrangement, and I would earnestly recommend that this portion of the Potawatomis shall continue to draw their distributive share of the Potawatomi annuities. The rights of nationality which they purchased from the Kickapoos were paid for out of their own money, and cost the Potawatomi nation nothing." Nozhakem's industrious followers paid $8,000 for the privilege of settling on the land of the Vermillion Kickapoos.[12]

The Kickapoo Prophet's charismatic personality had reaped a harvest of converts where Christian missionaries had failed; the Potawatomis were just as devout and pious as Kenekuk's other followers. Most importantly, they held fast to the idea that squandering tribal lands and possessions was a severe violation of the Great Spirit's commands. They too believed that the earth was sacred and that "mere men were forbidden to sell it." Eventually the Potawatomi cultural influence would predominate over that of the Kickapoos; Nozhakem assumed the spiritual leadership of the combined bands after Kenekuk's death, and many years later the majority of the prophet's adherents spoke only the Potawatomi language.[13]

The Potawatomis were valuable allies for the Vermillion Kickapoos, because the 1850s were as crucial and difficult as any period in the band's history. Although William Clark had promised in the Treaty of Castor Hill that the Kansas reservation would belong to the Vermillion people forever, by midcentury, as Kenekuk had foreseen, white settlers were poised to surge across the Missouri River. Pressures were mounting once again for the removal of the Indians. Compounding their difficulties, a smallpox epidemic spread panic among the several tribes in the region that is now eastern Kansas and Nebraska.

In the early spring of 1851, smallpox broke out among the tribes at the Great Nemaha agency, just to the north of the Vermillion Kickapoo reservation. By September most of the region's Indians had been infected by the disease; the Sacs and Foxes of the Mississippi, whose lands lay to the southwest of Kenekuk's reservation, lost about three-hundred souls to smallpox and to what the agent called the "flux," or dysentery. "This last named disease made its appearance about the time the Indians commenced using their green corn," Agent John R. Chenault reported, and "a number of grown persons died from it, and the mortality from it among the children was very great." Fortunately for the Kickapoos and Potawatomis, the Great Spirit, or simple blind luck, helped them avoid any serious illnesses during 1851. Agent William P. Richardson reported on September 17 that Kenekuk's followers "had the good fortune to escape the pestilence [smallpox] entirely, although it has spread to nearly all the neighboring tribes."[14]

The Indians of Kansas had need of strength and courage, for the waves of disease were followed by tides of white settlement flooding their lands. The Vermillion Kickapoos and Potawatomis, however, looked to the future with confidence, for Kenekuk had helped them to cement a strong tribal bond that would protect them in time of peril. They were unaware, in the autumn of 1851, that they were about to face their greatest crisis. For sometime during the following year, the dreaded smallpox apparently reached the Kickapoos and Potawatomis; the many dead included Kenekuk, their beloved prophet.

9. The Vermillion People Avoid the Ruinous Road

The precise date of the Kickapoo Prophet's death remains a mystery, for governmental officials and other whites initially paid little attention to the event. Agent William Richardson's September 1852 report to the superintendent of Indian Affairs in St. Louis stated merely that the Vermillion people had "lost Keu-e-kuck, their principal chief." The agent's apparent lack of interest was not really surprising; a year earlier, jurisdiction over the Kickapoos had been transferred from the Fort Leavenworth Agency to the Great Nemaha Agency, near the eastern border of present-day Kansas and Nebraska. The agents in charge at Great Nemaha—Richardson and his successor, David Vanderslice—knew little about the history or background of the Kickapoos. The agency was a considerable distance from Kenekuk's village, and neither agent had much contact with the Kickapoos and Potawatomis. Neither apparently had ever met Kenekuk!

Six years elapsed before another federal official mentioned Kenekuk's passing. In September 1859, Agent W. P. Badger, attempting to explain the failure of Christian missions to the Kickapoos, informed his superiors that Kenekuk's religion still held a powerful sway over the Indians. The greatest hindrance to the conversion of the Indians, Badger asserted, had been Kenekuk, "who for many years had been their prophet and leader, and who would not allow any innovation upon their original belief." The agent's account of the time and circumstances surrounding the prophet's death, however, was based on secondhand information: "Two or three years since, the small-pox terminated his existence with that of thirty or forty of his infatuated followers, who, remaining with his body after death, were desirous of witnessing his last prophecy, that 'in three days he would rise again.' "²

The most detailed account of Kenekuk's last hours was written by the Presbyterian missionary William Honnell, years after he had first visited the Kickapoos and Potawatomis in May 1857. Kenekuk and Mecina had been "conspicuous names among the Indians," Honnell recalled.

> The first had been a prophet and the second was a living chief of great influence among them. Kennekuk had died a few years before in style and grandeur, as become a prophet of the Great Spirit of the Indian race. He had become a half convert from his heathen incantations and exhorted his people to embrace the religion of Christ. He would relapse into heathenism again, and under censure of his Christian teachers would weep in such seeming penitence that he was restored to his office of Christian teacher to his tribe. His death in the log church on the Kickapoo village site near Fort Leavenworth was wierd and strange. He felt that death was near as he lay writhing and swollen with smallpox, the Indians' king of terrors. He had his followers to lay him out in the lone, silent church, that he might feel the presence of the great spirit in his dying hour. He muttered incantations and exhortations in turn, and told his deluded people that if he died, he would rise again, as Christ did, on the third day. He died, they waited to see him rise, and after three days,

amid the wildest dismay, he was left and the infected tribe scattered into the ravines and along the streams of water until one fourth of the nation died. Like some ancient king, he went to the spirit land accompanied or followed by an escort of warriors [and] women and children, composing a vast throng. Their bones, as left to bleach in the woods and in cabins, were often found after months had passed away. Thus died Kennekuk, the Prophet of the Kickapoos.[3]

Later accounts also mentioned that the Indians believed that Kenekuk, like Jesus Christ, would rise again after three days. In the late 1850s a seventeen-year-old girl named Hortense Kooken arrived in Kansas to serve as a teacher in a new Presbyterian school for the Kickapoos. Years later, Kooken told her daughter stories about the Indians, including one about the prophet's funeral, which she undoubtedly learned from Reverend Honnell. She too mentioned that the tribal members keeping vigil over Kenekuk's body had become "infested with smallpox [and] scattered up and down the valleys and ravines to their various villages. Many of them, not able to reach their homes, left their bones to bleach along the trails. Hundreds of Kickapoos died."[4]

Because there were only about four hundred and fifty Vermillion Kickapoos and Potawatomis, a catastrophe of such magnitude would have devastated the band. Official records, however, raise serious doubts as to the accuracy of such stories. Agent Richardson made no mention of smallpox in his 1852 report of Kenekuk's death; indeed, he thought the Indians were doing rather well and indicated no special concern about their health. "The past year [1852] may well be distinguished as one of remarkable quiet and repose among the Indians embraced within my jurisdiction," he wrote to his superiors.[5]

Like many whites who were acquainted with Kenekuk, Richardson had mixed feelings about the Kickapoo leader. The agent's brief eulogy praised the Indian for having commanded "a beneficial influence over a great portion of that tribe for some years before his death, in restraining, by all the means in his power, the introduction and use of spirits." Richardson also mentioned, however, that the prophet "was notorious for his superstitious quackery—a conjurer of the first water—and regarded by most of his people as possessing supernatural powers."[6]

Although ethnocentric and condescending, this view of the Kickapoo Prophet was partially accurate. The Vermillion people did believe that the Great Spirit spoke through Kenekuk and had given him special powers. These powers, however, were employed, not for personal gain, but to benefit the entire band. As a charismatic leader, Kenekuk had played a vital role in his followers' long quest to survive and prosper; his religion had cemented a firm community bond between the Kickapoos and the Potawatomis. Even his death did not disturb their work to ensure a secure future; they built cabins, planted crops, raised livestock, and sold surpluses for profit. They abstained from drinking, gambling, carousing, and other behavior that could not only have eroded their solidarity but also have brought disfavor from the white settlers who flooded into Kansas during the 1850s.

Their religious unity proved invaluable in their subsequent struggle against white encroachment on their lands and possessions. The prophet's adherents were ever willing to make diplomatic accommodation to the dominant American culture, but they never entirely capitulated to white pressure. They skillfully used their flexibility to defend against outside threats, and they maintained a separate Indian way of life within a white community.

They faced a difficult time after the loss of Kenekuk, who had been the heart and soul of their courageous stand to survive as a people. By the 1850s whites, who had once referred to lands beyond the Missouri River as the Great American Desert, realized that the region was well suited for farming. With citizens demanding that the federal government open the area for settlement, the commissioner of Indian Affairs obligingly negotiated new treaties with the Vermillion Kickapoos and other bands. In 1854 Kenekuk's people agreed to sell much of their reservation in exchange for governmental guarantees of protection on their reduced holdings. But almost immediately after they had agreed to the treaty, Congress passed the Kansas-Nebraska Act, and settlers, businessmen, and land speculators poured into the new Kansas Territory.

Thousands of settlers arrived during the 1850s and 1860s, and pressures increased on the Vermillion Band, as well as on the Prairie Potawatomis, Delawares, Osages, Shawnees, Sacs, Foxes, and others to move to Indian Territory (present-day Oklahoma). Successive administrations in Washington, preoccupied first with slavery and then with the Civil War and Reconstruction, showed little concern for a few thousand Indians in Kansas. Left to fend for themselves, most of the bands succumbed to the pressures and moved to Indian Territory.[7] But Kenekuk's religion had given the Vermillion Kickapoos and Potawatomis the strength to resist, and by the early 1870s they were among the few Indians left in Kansas.

Throughout the history of Indian-white relations in North America, there have been attempts by individual Indians to adapt their tribal cultures to meet the challenges of a changing world. In 1680 the prophet of the Pueblos, Popé, led a revolt that temporarily expelled the Spanish from New Mexico. Eighty-two years later, in Michigan, a Delaware prophet helped to instigate a holy war against Anglo-Americans. An Indian named Pontiac took over that movement and led a massive intertribal rebellion against the British and the American colonists. In the War of 1812 the Shawnee Prophet and Tecumseh forged a similar intertribal attack on the Americans. In the late nineteenth century, a Paiute named Wovoka reported that the Great Spirit had prescribed a new dance—the Ghost Dance—that would reunite Indians with their ancestors; the great tribes were to rise again to reclaim their lost traditions, cultures, and lands from the whites. Unlike Kenekuk's peaceful efforts, these and most of the many other Indian revitalization movements met with disaster. Violence against the powerful whites rarely proved to be a viable undertaking. The Spaniards reconquered the Pueblos in 1692, British troops eventually crushed Pontiac's rebellion, the Americans defeated the Indians and killed Tecumseh at the Battle of the Thames in 1813, and the United States Army massacred over one hundred Sioux ghost dancers in 1890.

Kenekuk's followers never resorted to violence to achieve their goals. The Kickapoo Prophet's religious tenets prohibited that course of action, and the peaceful ways of the Vermillion Kickapoos and Potawatomis benefited those Indians greatly. During the remaining years of the nineteenth century and to the present day, they have labored to win the respect and acceptance of their Kansas neighbors. Unified by the Kickapoo Prophet's teachings, however, they have never forgotten their tribal heritage, and their acceptance of white culture has always stopped short of assimilation. They had followed the path to success blazed by Kenekuk; they heeded his advice and obeyed the commands of the Great Spirit. "One step a day in the narrow path, is better than fifteen steps a day in the road to ruin," Kenekuk had once told them.[8] Because they listened to their religious leader, the Kickapoos and Potawatomis avoided the ruinous road.

Today the small Kickapoo reservation, one of only three Indian reservations remaining in the state of Kansas, suggests that Kenekuk's religion was proof against all white men's schemes to assimilate or to dispossess the Vermillion people. Although his triumphs did not come on the warpath, the Kickapoo Prophet's life and achievements should not be forgotten. Kenekuk, the messenger of the Great Spirit, was truly an American Indian patriot.

Notes

Chapter 1. Introduction

1. Parts of this introduction are based on articles that I have previously published: see "The Vermillion Kickapoos of Illinois: The Prophet Kenekuk's Peaceful Resistance to Indian Removal, 1819–1833," *Selected Papers in Illinois History, 1983* (Springfield: Illinois State Historical Society, 1985), pp. 28–38; and "Kenekuk, the Kickapoo Prophet: Acculturation without Assimilation," *American Indian Quarterly* 9 (Summer 1985): 295–307, republished in *American Indian Prophets: Religious Leaders and Revitalization Movements*, ed. Clifford E. Trafzer (Newcastle, Calif.: Sierra Oaks Publishing Co., 1986), pp. 57–69.

2. Alvin M. Josephy, Jr., *The Patriot Chiefs: A Chronicle of American Indian Resistance* (New York: Viking Press, 1961), pp. xiii–xiv.

3. These Indians were generally referred to as the Vermillion Kickapoos. They were actually several loosely allied bands that settled along the Wabash River in Indiana and along the Vermillion River in Illinois. The Kickapoo Prophet's name has been spelled in a number of ways—e.g., *The Columbia Encyclopedia* spells it Kanakuk—but I have opted for Kenekuk.

4. These words were spoken before an Indian and white audience at a Baptist meeting near Danville, Illinois, on July 17, 1831; see Gurdon S. Hubbard, "A Kickapoo Sermon," *Illinois Monthly Magazine* 1 (October 1831): 473–476.

5. *Chief* is a white term that implies that a leader has been accorded the highest rank or office and may have absolute control over his or her people. Indians had no such designation for their

leaders; individuals could choose to follow or to ignore any particular person in the tribe, regardless of that person's status, without any negative repercussions. The term *chief* will be used occasionally in this work, however, to identify persons of actual and significant influence within a tribe or band. Governmental officials, missionaries, and businessmen usually knew who these people were but sometimes avoided the influential men (and on rare occasions, women) who resisted their overtures. Instead, these whites designated those Indians who were willing to do the whites' bidding as *chiefs*. Quotation marks will be used to signify that a certain Indian was in reality a paper chief—a "chief" who may have accepted bribes or other favors in exchange for tribal lands and rightful possessions.

6. Henry Warner Bowden, *American Indians and Christian Missions: Studies in Cultural Conflict* (Chicago and London: University of Chicago Press, 1981), pp. 194–195.

Chapter 2. The Vermillion Band Kickapoos

1. Anthony F. C. Wallace defines such a revitalization movement as "a deliberate, organized, conscious effort to construct a more satisfying culture" ("Revitalization Movements," *American Anthropologist* 58 [April 1956]: 249–263).

2. Ethnologist Fred W. Voget would call the Vermillion Kickapoo movement "positive nativism"—an attempt to attain social "regeneration through a selective rejection, modification, and synthesis of both traditional and alien cultural components" ("The American Indian in Transition: Reformation and Accommodation," *American Anthropologist* 58 [April 1956]: 249–263).

3. Kickapoo tribal customs and history are discussed by Arrell M. Gibson in *The Kickapoos: Lords of the Middle Border* (Norman: University of Oklahoma Press, 1963), pp. 1–51; Charles Callender, Richard K. Pope, and Susan M. Pope, "Kickapoo," in *Handbook of North American Indians,* vol. 15: *Northeast*, ed. Bruce G. Trigger (Washington, D.C.: Smithsonian Institution, 1978), pp. 656–667; Joseph B. Herring, "Cultural and Economic

Resilience Among the Kickapoo Indians of the Southwest," *Great Plains Quarterly* 6 (Fall 1986): 263-275.

4. Thomas Forsyth to William Clark, January 15, 1827, in Emma Helen Blair, ed., *The Indian Tribes of the Upper Mississippi Valley and Region of the Great Lakes*, 2 vols. (Cleveland, Ohio: Arthur H. Clark Co., 1911), 1:204.

5. "Harrison's Address to Indian Council," August 12, 1802, in *Governor's Messages and Letters: Messages and Letters of William Henry Harrison*, ed. Logan Esarey, 2 vols. (Indianapolis: Indiana Historical Commission, 1922), 1:52-55; Benjamin Parke to Governor Thomas Posey, April 10, 1816, ibid., 2:723-724.

6. R. David Edmunds offers complete discussions of both the Shawnee Prophet and Tecumseh in two excellent books: *The Shawnee Prophet* (Lincoln: University of Nebraska Press, 1983) and *Tecumseh and the Quest for Indian Leadership* (Boston: Little, Brown & Co., 1984).

7. Gibson is unclear as to what branch of the Kickapoo tribe was most active militarily in the War of 1812 (*Kickapoos*, pp. 60-77); Callender, Pope, and Pope argue that the Prairie Kickapoos initially opposed Tecumseh, but they offer no substantiation for this contention ("Kickapoo," p. 622); for Prairie Kickapoo actions see William Henry Harrison to Secretary of War William Eustes, December 4, 1811, in *Governor's Messages and Letters*, 2:656-667, and George C. McVicker, "A Chapter in the Warfare against the Indians in Illinois during the Year of 1812," *Journal of the Illinois State Historical Society* 24 (July 1931): 342-343. For the activities of the Vermillion bands see Harrison to Eustes, June 6, 1811, and "Statement of William Brigham," in *Governor's Messages and Letters*, 2:512-513, 703-704.

8. Parke to Posey, December 7, 1814, *Governor's Messages and Letters*, 2:679.

9. For discussions of the differences in Indian and white land-use patterns see Peter A. Thomas, "Contrastive Subsistence Strategies and Land Use as Factors for Understanding Indian-White Relations in New England," *Ethnohistory* 23 (Winter 1976): 3-5, 14-15; Wilcomb E. Washburn, "The Moral and Legal Justification for Dispossessing the Indians," in *Seventeenth Century America: Essays in Colonial History*, ed. James Morton

Smith (New York: W. W. Norton & Co., 1972), pp. 22-26; William T. Hagan, "Justifying Dispossession of the Indian: The Land Use Argument," in *American Indian Environments: Ecological Issues in Native American History*, ed. Christopher Vecsey and Robert W. Venables (Syracuse, N.Y.: Syracuse University Press, 1980), pp. 65-68.

10. Indian Commissioners to the Secretary of War, September 9, 1816, in Clarence E. Carter, ed., *Territorial Papers of the United States*, vol. 17: *Illinois Territory, 1814-1818* (Washington, D.C.: Government Printing Office, 1950), pp. 387-389; Acting Secretary of War George Graham to Illinois Governor Ninian Edwards, February 28, 1817, and G. Graham to Edwards, November 1, 1817, in Ninian W. Edwards, *History of Illinois from 1778 to 1833; and Life and Times of Ninian Edwards* (Springfield: Illinois State Journal Co., 1870; reprint, New York: Arno Press, 1975), pp. 540-541, 545-546.

11. The peace treaty with the Prairie Kickapoos was concluded on September 2, 1815; see Charles J. Kappler, comp., *Indian Affairs: Laws and Treaties*, vol. 2: *Treaties* (Washington, D.C.: Government Printing Office, 1904), pp. 116-117; Edwards to Secretary of War William H. Crawford, June 3, 1816, in Carter, *Illinois Territory*, pp. 348-349.

12. Excerpts from the diary of Enoch Honeywell, in *Travel Accounts of Indiana, 1679-1961: A Collection of Observations by Wayfaring Foreigners, Itinerants, and Peripatetic Hoosiers,* ed. Shirley S. McCord (Bloomington: Indiana Historical Bureau, 1970), pp. 75-76.

13. Kappler, *Treaties*, p. 131.

14. David Thomas, *Travels through the Western Country in the Summer of 1816* (Darien, Conn.: Hafner Publishing Co., 1970), p. 181.

15. Commissioners to the Secretary of War, September 9, 1816, in Carter, *Illinois Territory*, p. 389.

16. "A Speech Delivered by Governor Posey, Agent for Indian Affairs, to Seven Hundred and Sixty Indians at Fort Harrison," November 22, 1816, in *Governor's Messages and Letters*, pp. 738-742. No direct evidence indicates that Kenekuk was there; but as one of

the leading men of the Vermillion bands, he probably attended the meeting and heard the speech.

17. *Edwardsville* (Ill.) *Spectator,* October 19, 1819.

18. G. Graham to Edwards, February 28, 1817, in Edwards, *History of Illinois*, pp. 540–541.

19. Edwards to G. Graham, May 12, 1817, in Carter, *Illinois Territory*, pp. 505–506. Although Edwards claimed that the Kickapoos had no legal right to the central Illinois lands, a state newspaper later admitted that the "title of the Kickapoos was indisputable" (*Edwardsville Spectator*, August 7, 1819).

20. Jerome O. Steffen breaks with scholars who find continuity between the ideas of Jeffersonians and the later Jacksonian advocates of Indian removal. According to Steffen, the acquisition of land and Indian assimilation were mutually dependent ideas in the minds of Jeffersonians such as William Clark. These men believed that if quick assimilation failed, removal to the West would provide enough time for the Indians to become civilized. Jacksonians, on the other hand, believed that the Indians were savages, incapable of advancement. Removal served the interests of politically powerful whites, and assimilation became a far-lesser priority. See Steffen, *William Clark: Jeffersonian Man on the Frontier* (Norman: University of Oklahoma Press, 1977), pp. 130–142, 166–168, 176. For an opposing view see Francis Paul Prucha, "Andrew Jackson's Indian Policy: A Reassessment," *Journal of American History* 56 (December 1969): 527–539.

21. G. Graham to Edwards, March 26, 1817, and Thomas L. McKenney to Edwards, January 17, 1818, in Edwards, *History of Illinois*, pp. 543–544, 546; "Letter of Auguste Chouteau," April 16, 1818, and Chouteau to Edwards, July 17, 1818, in *The Edwards Papers; being a portion of a collection of the letters, papers, and manuscripts of Ninian Edwards*, ed. E. B. Washburn (Chicago: Fergus Printing Co., 1884), pp. 141–144.

22. Ferdinand Ernst, "Edwardsville, Vandalia, and the Sangamon Country," in *Prairie State: Impressions of Illinois, 1673–1967, by Travelers and other Observers*, ed. Paul M. Angle (Chicago: University of Chicago Press, 1968), p. 74.

23. *Illinois Intelligencer* (Kaskaskia), January 13, 1819.

24. Excerpt from the diary of Frederick Hollman, quoted by Ernst in "Edwardsville, Vandalia, and the Sangamon Country," pp. 71–72.

25. Kappler, *Treaties*, pp. 182-183; *Edwardsville Spectator*, August 7, 1819.

26. Parke to Secretary of War John C. Calhoun, August 10, 1819, and Agent William Prince to Calhoun, August 12, 1819, Letters Received, Secretary of War, Bureau of Indian Affairs, record group 75, National Archives, Washington, D.C. (microcopy 271, roll 2). Hereinafter cited as Secretary of War, BIA, RG75, M271, R2.

27. Calhoun to Parke, September 8, 1819, Letters Sent, Secretary of War, BIA, RG75, M15, R4. The signatures of Little Duck and Kenekuk do not appear on the 1819 treaty (see Kappler, *Treaties*, p. 184).

28. Milo Custer, "Masheena," *Transactions of the Illinois State Historical Society*, 1911, pp. 116–117; Indian Agent Richard Graham to William Clark, January 15, 1825, LR, St. Louis Superintendency, BIA, RG75, M234, R747.

29. Milo Custer asserted incorrectly that Kenekuk signed the 1819 treaties ceding the Kickapoos' Illinois lands (see "Kannekuk or Keeanakuk: The Kickapoo Prophet," *Illinois State Historical Society Journal* 2 [April 1918]: 48). Following Custer's lead, other writers have made the same mistake; see, e.g., George A. Schultz, "Kennekuk, the Kickapoo Prophet," *Kansas History* 3 (Spring 1980): 38–39. It is important to note that Kenekuk did not sign any land-cession treaty until 1832.

Chapter 3. Instructed by the Great Spirit

1. Kappler, *Treaties*, p. 131.

2. On July 8, 1821, at a Kickapoo village near the Wabash River, John Tipton wrote in his journal of "thier [*sic*] chief Little Duck a little oald [*sic*] ill looking man" (see Nellie A. Robertson and Dorothy Riker, eds., *The John Tipton Papers*, Indiana Historical Collections, 3 vols. [Indianapolis: Indiana Historical Bureau, 1942], 1:275–276).

3. The *Illinois Monthly Magazine* reported in October 1831 that Kenekuk "appears to be about forty years of age; is over the ordinary size; and although an untutored savage, has much in his manner and personal appearance, to make him interesting" (see Hubbard, "A Kickapoo Sermon," p. 473).

4. The Kansas Kickapoos and Potawatomis related this version of Kenekuk's youth to the anthropologist James H. Howard during the early 1960s. They are quoted by Howard in "The Kenakuk Religion: An Early Nineteenth Century Revitalization Movement 140 Years Later," *Museum News* 26, no. 11/12 (November/December 1965): 3–5. Although Howard spelled the prophet's name Kenakuk throughout his article, I changed it to the more accepted Kenekuk in this block quotation for reasons of consistency; minor changes were also made in Howard's punctuation. Circumstantial evidence suggests that the "priest" may have been a Methodist minister.

5. In a written questionnaire submitted in 1906 by the amateur historian George J. Remsburg, the Rev. John Masquequa, a Kickapoo Indian who was head of the Kenekuk church at the time, reported that the prophet was twenty-five when he began preaching to his people. Since Kenekuk's signature appears on the Vermillion Band's 1816 treaty, one may assume that he had taken a position of some responsibility among his people by that time. The treaty, incidentally, was a peace agreement between the Indians and the United States. See "Questions answered by Rev. Masquequa," 1906, in the George J. Remsburg Collection, file 78:3, Manuscript Division (MsD), Kansas State Historical Society, Topeka. Kansas State Historical Society material hereinafter is cited in the form Remsburg Collection, KSHS. For the treaty, see Kappler, *Treaties*, p. 131.

6. The amateur historian Milo Custer visited John Masquequa in October 1906, at which time the Indian religious leader explained the doctrine of the Kickapoo Prophet. Masquequa was rather sketchy in relating the details, however, and Custer's version of their discussion is rather confused. The interpretation described here is based on my understanding of their conversations. See Milo Custer to George W. Martin, December 10, 1906, History—Indians—Kickapoo file, MsD, KSHS; and Custer, "Kan-

nekuk or Keeanakuk," pp. 48–56; also see W. Patton to Rev. C. Elliott, May 8, 1843, History—Indians—General, MsD, KSHS, a typed copy of a letter that was originally published in the *Western Christian Advocate*.

7. Charles Augustus Murray, *Travels in North America during the Years 1834, 1835, and 1836, Including a Summer Residence with the Pawnee Tribe of Indians . . .* , 2 vols. (London: Richard Bentley, 1839), 2:78.

8. William D. Smith to Rev. E. P. Swift, July 3, 1833, American Indian Correspondence, Collection of Missionary Letters, 1833–1893, Presbyterian Historical Society, Greenwood Press, Inc., microfilm, box 3, vol. 1, letter 5, hereinafter cited as Presbyterian Mission Letters, with box, volume, and letter numbers. Isaac McCoy, *History of Baptist Indian Missions* (Washington, D.C.: W. M. Morrison; and New York: H. & S. Raynor, 1840), p. 457; Benedict Roux to Bishop Rosati, November 24, 1833, in Gilbert J. Garraghan, "Selected Letters from the Roux Correspondence," *Catholic Historical Review* 4 (April 1918): 92.

9. For descriptions of Kenekuk's services see John Dunbar and Samuel Allis, "Letters Concerning the Presbyterian Mission in the Pawnee Country, Near Bellevue, Neb., 1831–1849," *Collections of the Kansas State Historical Society* 14 (1918): 586; Custer to George Remsberg, December 8, 1908, the George J. Remsberg Collection, file 78:3, MsD, KSHS.

10. Murray, *Travels in North America*, pp. 78–80.

11. Hubbard, "A Kickapoo Sermon," pp. 473–476.

12. There are several similar accounts of the Kickapoo flagellation ceremony. Isaac McCoy, for example, also reported that after each Indian had "received the flagellation, which often brought blood, the penitent would shake hands with the executioner, and others near, returning thanks for the favour done him, and declaring that he felt relieved of a heavy burden" (*History of Baptist Indian Missions*, p. 458). Also see Jerome C. Berryman, "A Circuit-Rider's Frontier Experiences," *Collections of the Kansas State Historical Society* 16 (1923–1925): 216; Thomas Forsyth, "The Kickapoo Prophet," in *Indian Tribes of the Upper Mississippi Valley*, 1:280–281. For Hopkins's account see E. Duir, *The Good Old*

Times in McLean County, Illinois (Illinois: McKnight & McKnight Publishing Co., 1968), pp. 677–680.

13. For descriptions of the Kickapoo prayer sticks, see Murray, *Travels in North America*, p. 79; Dunbar and Allis, "Letters Concerning the Presbyterian Mission," p. 586; Remsburg to Custer, December 8, 1908, Remsburg Collection, 78:3, KSHS; Howard, "The Kenakuk Religion," pp. 23–26; Patton to Elliott, May 8, 1843, History—Indians—General, KSHS.

14. The anthropologist James Mooney wrote that the markings "bear some resemblance to the old black-letter type of a [Catholic] missal, while the peculiar arrangement is suggestive of the Catholic rosary with its fifteen 'mysteries' in three groups of five each." Mooney pointed out that neither three nor five were traditional Indian numbers, "while three is distinctly Christian in its symbolism" (*The Ghost-Dance Religion and Wounded Knee* [New York: Dover Publications, Inc., 1973], p. 699).

15. Smith to Swift, July 3, 1833, Presbyterian Mission Letters, box 3, vol. 1, letter 5; McCoy, *History of Baptist Indian Missions*, pp. 457–458.

16. Smith to Swift, July 3, 1833, Presbyterian Mission Letters, box 3, vol. 1, letter 5.

17. For discussions on the persistence of traditional customs see George J. Remsburg, "Some Notes on the Kickapoo Indians," *Philatelic West* 36 (1907): 325–326; Howard, "The Kenakuk Religion," pp. 38–40; Murray, *Travels in North America*, p. 78; Smith to Swift, July 3, 1833, Presbyterian Mission Letters, box 3, vol. 1, letter 5.

18. "Minutes of a Talk of the Kickapoo Prophet," May 24, 1828, LR, St. Louis Superintendency, BIA, RG75, M234, R748.

Chapter 4. Protector of His People's Rights

1. "Minutes of a Talk of the Kickapoo Prophet," May 24, 1828, LR, St. Louis Superintendency, BIA, RG75, M234, R748.

2. Kenekuk's talk is quoted by Mooney in *The Ghost-Dance Religion*, pp. 694–696, and by Howard in "The Kenakuk Religion," pp. 8–12.

3. William Clark to Richard Graham, October 22, 1823, Richard Graham Papers, box 3–12, Missouri Historical Society Archives, St. Louis, hereinafter cited as Graham Papers, with box numbers.

4. The description of Kenekuk is by John Treat Irving in *Indian Sketches, Taken during an Expedition to the Pawnee Tribes* (1833), ed. John Francis McDermott (Norman: University of Oklahoma Press, 1955), p. 43.

5. Francis Paul Prucha discusses nineteenth-century justifications for dispossessing eastern tribes in *American Indian Policy in the Formative Years: The Indian Trade and Intercourse Acts, 1790–1834* (Lincoln: University of Nebraska Press, 1973), pp. 239–242.

6. "Incidents of Frontier Life," *Journal of the Illinois State Historical Society* 32 (December 1939): 529.

7. John Tipton to Lewis Cass, October 31, 1823, *John Tipton Papers*, p. 323; Graham to Calhoun, June 21, 1821, Graham Papers, box 2–12.

8. Arrell Gibson maintains that Mecina and his followers "were diehard fanatics, choleric and troublesome, and for over a decade they defied the United States to evict them from their village near the head of Peoria Lake" (*Kickapoos*, p. 83). Richard Graham and other agents stated frequently, however, that Mecina and the Prairie Kickapoos were generally peaceful. Indeed, it was the white settlers who caused most of the trouble.

9. Maj. Morrell Marston to Rev. Jedidiah Morse, November 1820, in Blair, *Indian Tribes of the Upper Mississippi Valley*, p. 156. The citizens' petition is quoted by Gibson in *Kickapoos*, pp. 84–85.

10. For Mecina's response to white intruders see Milo Custer, "Masheena," pp. 116-117; and Duir, *Good Old Times in McLean County*, pp. 174-175. Also see A. F. Hubbard to Clark, October 27, 1825, *Collections of the Illinois State Historical Library* 4 (1909): 91–92.

11. Graham to Clark, January 15, 1825, and "Talk of Mecina of Kickapoos to Graham," January 15, 1825, LR, St. Louis Superintendency, BIA, RG75, M234, R747. Copies of these letters can also be found in the Graham Papers, box 3–12.

12. For a description of the Pine Creek village see *John Tipton Papers*, pp. 275–276.

13. Graham to Clark, February 22, 1827, in Mooney, *Ghost-Dance Religion*, pp. 693–694.

14. Ibid., p. 694.

15. James B. Ray to the President, November 25, 1825, *Messages and Papers Relating to the Administration of James Brown Ray, Governor of Indiana, 1825–1831*, ed. Dorothy Riker and Gayle Thornbrough (Indianapolis: Indiana Historical Bureau, 1954), pp. 57–58.

16. Secretary of War James Barbour to Ray, January 28, 1826, ibid., p. 116.

17. Edwards to the Secretary of War, August 20, 1827, in *Edwards Papers*, pp. 298–300.

18. Edwards to the Secretary of War, September 4, 1827, ibid., pp. 306–310.

19. Edwards to Barbour, October 29, 1827, in Edwards, *History of Illinois*, pp. 355–356.

20. Graham to Clark, November 8, 1827, and Clark to the Secretary of War, November 15, 1827, LR, St. Louis Superintendency, BIA, RG75, M234, R748; for information on Kickapoo locations in Illinois, which is not necessarily accurate, see H. W. Beckwith and J. H. Burnham, *An Ancient Indian Fort: Some Accounts of Its History, with an Outline of the Works* (Bloomington, Ill.: Pantagraph Printing Establishment, 1881), pp. 6–8.

21. "Talk by Major R. Graham, Indian agent to the Kickapoo in Illinois," November 23, 1827, LR, St. Louis Superintendency, BIA, RG75, M234, R748.

22. Clark to Barbour, November 15, 1827, ibid.

23. Descriptions of this ceremony can be found in Custer, "Masheena," pp. 117–118; and Duir, *Good Old Times in McLean County*, pp. 174-175. David Evans provides an astute analysis of the different aesthetics of Indian culture and music in "North American Indian Music," *Journal of American Folklore* 90 (July-September 1977): 364–365.

24. A valuable source of pertinent information, such as the arrival of Indian delegations, the weather, and other data, can be

found in ed. Louise Barry, "William Clark's Diary: May, 1826–February, 1831," *Kansas Historical Quarterly* 16 (May 1848): 136-174.

25. "In council with the Kickapoos of Illinois," May 18, 1828, LR, St. Louis Superintendency, BIA, RG75, M234, R748.

26. Ibid.

27. "Minutes of a talk of the Kickapoo Prophet," May 24, 1828, ibid.

28. Clark to Edwards, May 26, 1828, ibid.

29. Edwards to Clark, May 25 and 29, 1828, *Edwards Papers*, pp. 338-340.

30. Letter of William Clark, June 1, 1828, LR, St. Louis Superintendency, BIA, RG75, M234, R748.

31. Peter B. Porter to Edwards, July 7 and 22, 1828, *Collections of the Illinois State Historical Library* 4 (1909): 139.

32. For an evaluation of McCoy's motives see George A. Schultz, *An Indian Canaan: Isaac McCoy and the Vision of an Indian State* (Norman: University of Oklahoma Press, 1972); also see Lela Barnes, ed., "Journal of Isaac McCoy for the Exploring Expedition of 1828," *Kansas Historical Quarterly* 5 (August 1936): 227-277; Roscoe Wilmeth, "Kansa Village Locations in Light of McCoy's 1828 Journal," ibid., 26 (Summer 1960): 152-157; John Francis McDermott, ed., "Isaac McCoy's Second Exploring Trip in 1828," ibid., 13 (August 1945): 400-462; Barnes, "Journal of Isaac McCoy," pp. 339-377.

33. "In Council with the Kickapoos of Illinois," May 18, 1828, and "Council with the Kickapoo," June 13, 1836, LR, St. Louis Superintendency, BIA, RG75, M234, R748 and R751.

Chapter 5. The Storms of War and Removal

1. Hubbard, "A Kickapoo Sermon," p. 473.

2. William T. Hagan, *The Sac and Fox Indians* (Norman: University of Oklahoma Press, 1958), pp. 16-47.

3. Anthony F. C. Wallace discusses these events in *Prelude to Disaster: The Course of Indian-White Relations Which Led to the*

Black Hawk War of 1832 (Springfield: Illinois State Historical Library, 1970), pp. 30–31.

4. There are many scholarly studies on the background, process, and aftermath of Jackson's Indian removal policy: see, for example, Annie H. Abel, "The History of Events Resulting in Indian Consolidation West of the Mississippi," in *Annual Report of the American Historical Association for the Year 1906* (1908), vol. 1, pp. 233–450; R. David Edmunds, "The Prairie Potawatomi Removal of 1833," *Indiana Magazine of History* 68 (September 1972): 240–253; Grant Foreman, *The Last Trek of the Indians* (Chicago: University of Chicago Press, 1946); Reginald Horsman, *The Origins of Indian Removal, 1815–1824* (East Lansing: Michigan State University Press, 1970); Dale Van Every, *Disinherited: The Lost Birthright of the American Indian* (New York: Avon Books, 1966); Wilcomb E. Washburn, "Indian Removal Policy: Administrative, Historical and Moral Criteria for Judging Its Success or Failure," *Ethnohistory* 12 (Summer 1965): 274–278; Mary E. Young, "Indian Removal and Land Allotment: The Civilized Tribes and Jacksonian Justice," *American Historical Review* 64 (October 1958): 31–45.

5. Quoted by Francis Paul Prucha in "Andrew Jackson's Indian Policy," in *The Indian in American History*, ed. Prucha (Hinsdale, Ill.: Dryden Press, 1971), p. 73.

6. These words of an old Choctaw chief are quoted by Michael Paul Rogin in *Fathers and Children: Andrew Jackson and the Subjugation of the American Indian* (New York: Vantage Books, 1976), p. 209.

7. See Francis Paul Prucha, "Thomas L. McKenney and the New York Indian Board," *Mississippi Valley Historical Review* 48 (March 1962): 635–655; Herman J. Viola, *Thomas L. McKenney: Architect of America's Early Indian Policy, 1816–1830* (Chicago: Swallow Press, 1974).

8. Viola, *Thomas L. McKenney*, p. 216.

9. For information on McKenney and the New York Board see Ronald N. Satz, *American Indian Policy in the Jacksonian Era* (Lincoln: University of Nebraska Press, 1975), pp. 15–20.

10. For McCoy's role see William Miles, " 'Enamoured with Colonization': Isaac McCoy's Plan for Indian Reform," *Kansas Historical Quarterly* 38 (Autumn 1972): 268–286.

11. Quoted by Bernard W. Sheehan in *Seeds of Extinction: Jeffersonian Philanthropy and the American Indian* (New York: W. W. Norton & Co., 1974), p. 252.

12. For a detailed discussion of the missionary view of Indians and the idea that contact with lower classes of whites hindered Indian social development see Robert F. Berkhofer, Jr., *Salvation and the Savage: An Analysis of Protestant Missions and American Indian Response, 1787–1862* (New York: Atheneum, 1976), pp. 99–106.

13. Quoted in Rogin, *Fathers and Children*, p. 217.

14. Quoted in Satz, *American Indian Policy in the Jacksonian Era*, p. 20.

15. For Jackson's thoughts on the bill see ibid., pp. 19–20; and "Message of Andrew Jackson to the Two Houses of Congress," 21st Cong., 2d sess., *Senate Documents*, ser. 203 (1832), p. 19.

16. Quoted by Sheehan in *Seeds of Extinction*, p. 274.

17. Quoted by Rogin in *Fathers and Children*, p. 231.

18. The quotes are from Satz, *American Indian Policy in the Jacksonian Era*, pp. 107–108.

19. Quoted by Prucha in "Andrew Jackson's Indian Policy," p. 74.

20. Quoted from Hubbard, "A Kickapoo Sermon," pp. 473–476. Minor changes have been made in the punctuation of the original sermon.

21. William M. Hendrix to E. M. Prince, November 28, 1897, Remsburg Collection, MsD, KSHS.

22. George Catlin, *Letters and Notes on the Manners, Customs, and Conditions of the North American Indians*, 2 vols. (New York: Dover Publications, Inc., 1973), 2:97–99.

23. Wallace, *Prelude to Disaster*, pp. 36–38.

24. Arrell Gibson suggests that these Kickapoos were part of Mecina's people, but he offers little evidence to support his conclusion (see *Kickapoos*, pp. 86–87). The Kickapoos were a highly independent and mobile tribe during the nineteenth century, however, and these particular Indians could have just as eas-

ily come from Missouri or other locations to join Black Hawk.

25. Virtually all of the Kickapoo men associated with Black Hawk were killed during the war (see "The Minutes of the Examination of Prisoners of the Black Hawk War," LR, Secretary of War, Unregistered Series, RG107, M222, R31).

26. *Vandalia Whig and Illinois Intelligencer*, June 13, 1832; *St. Louis Beacon*, May 31, 1832.

27. Winfield Scott to Lewis Cass, August 19, 1832, LR, Secretary of War, RG107, M222, R31; Agent William Marshall signed a pass to allow Kenekuk and his people to hunt on federal lands, dated July 5, 1832, see the Remsburg Collection, 78:3, KSHS; *St. Joseph* (Ind.) *Beacon*, June 6, 1832, quoted by Ella Lonn in "Ripples of the Black Hawk War in Northern Indiana," *Indiana Magazine of History* 20 (Sept. 1924): 303-304.

28. Clark to Kenekuk, August 31, 1832 and January 31, 1833, both in the Remsburg Collection, 78:3, and the History—Indians—Kickapoo file, KSHS.

29. Kappler, *Treaties*, pp. 365-367.

30. Forsyth, "Kickapoo Prophet," pp. 280-281.

31. Clark to Kenekuk, January 16, 1833, History—Indians—Kickapoo file, KSHS.

Chapter 6. Kenekuk's Village on the Missouri

1. Irving, *Indian Sketches*, pp. 39-41.

2. Charles F. Hoffman, *A Winter in the West, by a New Yorker* (New York: Harper & Brothers, 1835), pp. 82-85; Dunbar and Allis, "Letters Concerning the Presbyterian Mission," p. 693.

3. Elbert Herring to William Clark, June 3, 1833, Letters Sent, Office of Indian Affairs, BIA, RG75, M21, R10.

4. Quoted by Gibson in *Kickapoos*, p. 111.

5. Herring to M. Stokes, H. L. Ellsworth, and J. F. Schermerhorn, June 1, 1833, 23rd Cong., 1st sess., *Senate Documents*, ser. 247 (1833), pp. 706-707.

6. Irving, *Indian Sketches*, p. 38.

7. Ibid., p. 40.

8. Ibid., pp. 41-42.

9. Ibid., p. 42.

10. Ibid., pp. 42–43.

11. A council between Henry Ellsworth and the Kickapoos, September 2, 1833, LR, Western Superintendency, BIA, RG75, M234, R921. A transcript of this council can also be found in 23rd Cong., 1st sess., *Senate Documents*, ser. 247 (1833), pp. 640–643.

12. Ibid.

13. The Kickapoos and whites who attended the council referred to this river as the Osage. Actually, it is the same river as the Marais des Cygnes; in Missouri it is called the Osage, but in Kansas it is now called the Marais des Cygnes (river of swans).

14. Council between Ellsworth and the Kickapoos, September 2, 1833, LR, Western Superintendency, BIA, RG75, M234, R921.

15. Ellsworth to Herring, November 8, 1833, LR, Fort Leavenworth Agency, ibid., R300; Ellsworth to Herring, November [?], 1833, and "A Second Talk with the Kickapoos and Potawatomis at Fort Leavenworth," November 13, 1833, LR, Western Superintendency, ibid., R921. Some of Henry Ellsworth's correspondence was signed by his son Edward A. Ellsworth, secretary pro tem.

16. Verhaegen is quoted by Louise Callan in *Philippine Duchesne: Frontier Missionary of the Sacred Heart, 1769–1852* (Westminster, Md.: Newman Press, 1957), pp. 625–626.

17. Richard Cummins to Clark, April 20, 1834, LR, Fort Leavenworth Agency, BIA, RG75, M234, R300.

18. Cummins to Herring, September 30, 1835, and Capt. Matthew Duncan to Col. Henry Dodge, May 23, 1835, ibid.

19. Ibid.

20. Count Francesco Arese, *A Trip to the Prairies and in the Interior of North America [1837–1838]* (New York: Cooper Square Publishers, Inc., 1975), pp. 65–66.

21. "Council with the Kickapoos," June 13, 1836, and Duncan to Gen. Henry Atkinson, June 14, 1836, LR, St. Louis Superintendency, BIA, RG75, M234, R751.

22. Clark was not present at the council.

23. "Council with the Kickapoos," June 13, 1836, and Duncan to Gen. Henry Atkinson, June 14, 1836, LR, St. Louis Superintendency, BIA, RG75, M234, R751.

24. Ibid.

25. Duncan to Atkinson, June 14, 1836, and Atkinson to Gen. R. Jones, June 28, 1836, ibid.; Clark to Herring, July 8, 1836, LR, Fort Leavenworth Agency, ibid., R300.

26. McCoy, *History of Baptist Indian Missions*, p. 458; Nathaniel Talbott to Thomas B. Sargent and John Davis, May 29, 1843, LR, Fort Leavenworth Agency, BIA, RG75, M234, R302; David Kinnear to Cummins, September 30, 1838, ibid., R301; Samuel Mason to Congressman John C. Mason, December 26, 1849, ibid., R303.

27. Cummins to Clark, January 31 and May 16, 1838, and Cummins to Commissioner of Indian Affairs C. A. Harris, September 25, 1838, ibid., R301.

28. Cummins to Superintendent of Indian Affairs at St. Louis Joshua Pilcher, October [?], 1839, 26th Cong., 1st sess., *Senate Documents*, ser. 354 (1839), p. 502.

29. "Talk by Kickapoo Chiefs," December 31, 1838, LR, Fort Leavenworth Agency, BIA, RG75, M234, R301.

30. Cummins to Pilcher, October [?], 1839, 26th Cong., 1st sess., *Senate Documents,* ser. 354 (1839), p. 501; Gilbert J. Garraghan, "The Kickapoo Mission," *St. Louis Catholic Historical Review* 4 (January–April 1922): 47.

Chapter 7. Kenekuk and the Missionaries

1. McCoy, *History of Baptist Indian Missions*, pp. 456–457.

2. Smith to Swift, July 3, 1833, Presbyterian Mission Letters, box 3, vol. 1, letter 5.

3. Harriet Livermore, *A Narration of Religious Experience, in Twelve Letters*, 2 vols. (Concord, N.H.: Printed by Jacob B. Moore for the author, 1826), 1:30; also see Elizabeth F. Hoxie, "Harriet Livermore: 'Vixen and Devotee,'" *New England Quarterly* 18 (March 1945): 40–41.

4. Hoxie, "Harriet Livermore," pp. 40–45; Arthur M. Schlesinger, "Casting the National Horoscope," *Proceedings of the American Antiquarian Society* 55 (April 1947): 56; Madison is quoted by Virginia Moore in *The Madisons: A Biography* (New York: McGraw-Hill Book Co., 1979), p. 418; John G. Whittier to

a friend, September 18, 1879, *The Letters of John Greenleaf Whittier*, vol. 3, *1861–1892*, ed. John B. Pickard (Cambridge, Mass.: Belknap Press of Harvard University Press, 1975), pp. 412–413; *Memoirs of John Quincy Adams, Comprising Portions of His Diary from 1795 to 1848*, 12 vols., ed. Charles Francis Adams (Freeport, N.Y.: Books for Libraries Press, 1969), 10:6–7.

5. H. Livermore, *Narration of Religious Experience*, p. 13.

6. In 1829, Livermore wrote to former President James Madison, asking his assistance in her project to free Charleston's slaves (see Livermore to James Madison, October 22, 1829, *James Madison Papers*, ser. 1, reel 22, Presidential Papers Microfilm, Library of Congress, Washington, D.C.).

7. S. T. Livermore, *Harriet Livermore the "Pilgrim Stranger"* (Hartford, Conn.: Lockwood & Brainard Co., 1884), pp. 123–126; Harriet Livermore, *Millennial Tidings* (Philadelphia: The Author, 1839), p. 5; Harriet Livermore, *The Harp of Israel to Meet the Loud Echo in the Wilds of America* (Philadelphia: J. Rakestraw, 1835), pp. 3–5.

8. H. Livermore, *Millennial Tidings*, p. 5; H. Livermore, *A Letter to John Ross, the Principle Chief of the Cherokee Nation* (Philadelphia: The Author, 1838), p. 11.

9. See both citations in notes 8, above.

10. Ellsworth to Herring, August 19, 1833, LR, Western Superintendency, BIA, RG75, M234, R921; H. Livermore, *Letter to John Ross*, p. 6.

11. Ellsworth to Herring, August 19, 1833, LR, Western Superintendency, BIA, RG75, M234, R921.

12. Ibid.

13. S. T. Livermore, *Harriet Livermore the "Pilgrim Stranger,"* pp. 123–124; H. Livermore, *Harp of Israel*, pp. 5–6.

14. Roux is quoted in Gilbert J. Garraghan, *Catholic Beginnings in Kansas City, Missouri: An Historical Sketch* (Chicago: Loyola University Press, 1920), pp. 49–54, and "Selected Letters from the Roux Correspondence," p. 92, and "Kickapoo Mission," p. 26.

15. Quoted by J. J. Lutz in "The Methodist Missions among the Indian Tribes in Kansas," *Transactions of the Kansas State Historical Society* 9 (1905/1906): 208–209.

16. Berryman, "A Circuit-Rider's Frontier Experiences," pp. 215–216. This article has been reprinted in William W. Sweet, *Religion on the American Frontier, 1783–1840*, vol. 4: *The Methodists: A Collection of Source Materials* (New York: Cooper Square Publishers, Inc., 1964), p. 538.

17. The school opened on March 4, 1834; see Berryman, "A Circuit-Rider's Frontier Experiences," pp. 523–525; a Letter of Berryman, January 28, 1835, typed copy from the *Christian Advocate and Journal* 9 (March 13, 1835): 114, History—Indians—General, KSHS.

18. Dunbar and Allis, "Letters Concerning the Presbyterian Mission," p. 586.

19. Samuel Allis to Rev. David Green, May 12, 1835, in Dunbar and Allis, "Letters Concerning the Presbyterian Mission," p. 695. A few corrections in punctuation and spelling have been made in this passage for the sake of clarity. For the most part, however, Allis's writing (including errors in spelling) is reproduced verbatim.

20. Berryman, "A Circuit-Rider's Frontier Experiences," p. 216.

21. Thomas Johnson to the Corresponding Secretary of the Methodist Episcopal Church, June 16, 1836, in Sweet, *Religion on the American Frontier*, pp. 516–518.

22. For an excellent analysis of Jesuit attitudes, see Edward H. Spicer, *Cycles of Conquest: The Impact of Spain, Mexico, and the United States on the Indians of the Southwest, 1533*–1960 (Tucson: University of Arizona Press, 1962), pp. 308–324. For other discussions of Jesuit attitudes and methods see Peter Duignan, "Early Jesuit Missionaries: A Suggestion for Further Study," *American Anthropologist* 60 (August 1958): 725–732; James P. Ronda, "The European Indian: Jesuit Civilization Planning in New France," *Church History* 41 (September 1972): 388–393.

23. Charles F. Van Quickenborne wrote about this exchange with Kenekuk in "Relation d'un voyage fait chez les tribus indiennes situées à l'ouest du Missouri," September 24, 1835, *Annales de la propagation de la foi* 9 (September 1836): 99–101. For an English translation see Gilbert J. Garraghan, *The Jesuits of the Middle United States*, 3 vols. (New York: America Press, 1938), 1:388–389, and "Kickapoo Mission," pp. 27–28.

24. See all citations in notes 23, above.

25. Ibid.

26. See Van Quickenborne to Cass, September 17, 1835, Herring to Van Quickenborne, September 22, 1835, and Van Quickenborne to Bishop Rosati, in Garraghan, *Jesuits of the Middle United States*, pp. 390–392.

27. Van Quickenborne to Father William McSherry, June 29, 1836, ibid., pp. 395–397.

28. Peter Verhaegen to McSherry, July 10, 1836, and Van Quickenborne to McSherry, June 29, 1836, ibid., pp. 404–405, 397.

29. Verhaegan, "Report of the Teacher for the Kickapoos," 1837, 25th Cong., 2 sess. *Senate Documents*, ser. 314 (1837), pp. 571–572.

30. "Council with the Kickapoos," June 13, 1836, LR, St. Louis Superintendency, BIA, RG75, M234, R751.

31. Garraghan, *Jesuits of the Middle United States*, p. 406, and "Kickapoo Mission," pp. 37–40.

32. Verhaegen, "Report on the Indian Missions to the Most Rev. Archbishop and Right Rev. Bishops in the Provincial Council Assembled," 1841, and Verhaegen to the Secretary of War, November 5, 1837, in Garraghan, *Jesuits of the Middle United States*, pp. 406–407 n. 56 and 414–415.

33. Quoted by Garraghan in *Jesuits of the Middle United States*, p. 418. Although Pashishi mentioned that the Jesuits "cured" his people of smallpox, a government-employed doctor certified that most of the Kickapoos had been vaccinated by Berryman, the Methodist missionary (see J. A. Chute to Cummins, July 23, 1838, LR, Fort Leavenworth Agency, BIA, RG75, M234, R301).

34. Pierre Jean De Smet, *Life, Letters, and Travels of Father Pierre-Jean De Smet, S.J., 1801–1873. . .*, 4 vols., ed. Hiram M. Chittenden and Alfred T. Richardson (New York: Francis P. Harper, 1905; reprint New York: Kraus Reprint Co., 1969), 1:150–151, 162.

35. Berryman to Cummins, October (?), 1839, LR, St. Louis Superintendency, BIA, RG75, M234, R752, and Berryman to Cummins, August 15, 1842, 27th Cong., 3d sess., *Senate Documents,* ser. 413 (1842), pp. 488–489.

36. Berryman, "A Circuit-Rider's Frontier Experiences," pp. 216–217.

37. Cummins to Superintendent of Indian Affairs at St. Louis Joshua Pilcher, October [?], 1839, LR, St. Louis Superintendency, BIA, RG75, M234, R752.

38. Point is quoted by Garraghan in *Jesuits of the Middle United States*, pp. 418–420.

39. De Smet, *Life, Letters, and Travels*, 1:150–151, 3:1085–1086.

40. Patton to Elliott, May 8, 1843, History—Indians—General, MsD, KSHS.

41. Talbott to Sargent and Davis, May 29, 1843, LR, Fort Leavenworth Agency, BIA, RG75, M234, R302; Patton to Elliott, May 8, 1843, History—Indians—General, MsD, KSHS.

42. Wright is quoted by Louise Barry in *The Beginning of the West: Annals of the Kansas Gateway to the American West, 1540–1854* (Topeka: Kansas State Historical Society, 1972), p. 1066.

Chapter 8. A Successful Future Assured

1. "Talk by Kickapoo Chiefs," December 31, 1838, LR, Fort Leavenworth Agency, BIA, RG75, M234, R301.

2. Cummins to St. Louis Superintendent of Indian Affairs D. D. Mitchell, September 12, 1842, 27th Cong., 3d sess., *Senate Documents*, ser. 413, (1842), p. 436; Cummins to Mitchell, October 1, 1843, 28th Cong., 1st sess., *Senate Documents*, ser. 431, (1843), p. 404; Superintendent of Indian Affairs Thomas Harvey to Commissioner William Medill, November 17, 1846, LR, Fort Leavenworth Agency, BIA, RG75, M234, R302.

3. Cummins to Mitchell, July 22, 1841, and June 23, 1842, LR, Fort Leavenworth Agency, BIA, RG75, M234, R301.

4. Cummins to Mitchell, June 22, 1843, Talbott to Sargent and Davis, May 29, 1843, and Harvey to the Commissioner of Indian Affairs, February 21, 1846, ibid., R302.

5. Cummins to Harvey, March 25, 1844, ibid.

6. "Potawatomi petition to remain with the Kickapoos," June 8, 1844, ibid.

7. Harvey to Commissioner Thomas Hartley Crawford, June 8, 1844, ibid.

8. Nozhakem and other Potawatomi chiefs to the Commis-

sioner, December 22, 1849, and Samuel Mason to John C. Mason, December 26, 1849, ibid., R303.

9. Maj. B. F. Roberts to E. F. Sumner, Commander at Fort Leavenworth, February 13, 1849, and a petition signed by Kenekuk, Mecina, and others, December 8, 1850, ibid.

10. A petition signed by Kenekuk, Mecina, and Black Thunder in the presence of John Collier, February 8, 1851, ibid.

11. A petition by the Potawatomi chiefs in the presence of John Collier, February 8, 1851, and Collier to Mitchell, February 10, 1851, ibid.

12. Mitchell to Commissioner of Indian Affairs Luke Lea, October 25, 1851, 32d Cong., 1st sess., *Senate Documents*, ser. 613 (1852), p. 323; "Keotuck on behalf of the Potawatomies living on the Kickapoo Reserve," February 27, 1857, History—Indians—Potawatomi file, MsD, KSHS.

13. Howard, "The Kenakuk Religion," pp. 36–38.

14. John R. Chenault to Commissioner of Indian Affairs Luke Lea, September 17, 1851, and William P. Richardson to Mitchell, September 26, 1851, 32d Cong., 1st sess., *Senate Documents*, ser. 613 (1852), pp. 328–329, 361.

Chapter 9. The Vermillion People Avoid the Ruinous Road

1. Richardson to D. D. Mitchell, January 31, 1852, and David Vanderslice to A. Cumming, Superintendent at St. Louis, June 30, 1853, LR, Great Nemaha Agency, BIA, RG75, M234, R308.

2. Richardson to Mitchell, September 30, 1852, 32d Cong., 2d sess., *Senate Documents*, ser. 658 (1852), p. 361; W. P. Badger to Superintendent A. M. Robinson, September 20, 1859, 36th Cong., 1st sess., *Senate Documents*, ser. 1023 (1860), p. 144.

3. William H. Honnell, "A Glimpse at the early settlement of N.E. Kansas," no date, History—Indians—Kickapoo, MsD, KSHS.

4. Kooken told this story to her daughter Louise Green Hoad many years after Kenekuk had died. It was not until the 1940s that Hoad retold the events surrounding the prophet's death in her book *Kickapoo Indian Trails* (Caldwell, Idaho: Caxton Printers, Ltd., 1946), pp. 51–53.

5. Richardson to Mitchell, September 30, 1852, 32d Cong., 2d sess., *Senate Documents*, ser. 658 (1852), p. 360.

6. Ibid., p. 361.

7. An excellent account of the dispossession of tribal lands in Kansas can be found in H. Craig Miner and William E. Unrau, *The End of Indian Kansas: A Study of Cultural Revolution, 1854-1871* (Lawrence: Regents Press of Kansas, 1978), pp. 1-24, 55-106.

8. Quoted by Hubbard in "A Kickapoo Sermon," p. 475.

Bibliography

Manuscript Materials

National Archives

Record Group 75. M15. Letters Sent by the Secretary of War Relating to Indian Affairs, 1822–1823. R4.
_____. M21. Letters Sent by the Office of Indian Affairs, January–June 1833. R10.
_____. M234. Letters Received by the Office of Indian Affairs, Fort Leavenworth Agency, 1824–1851. R300-303.
_____. M234. Great Nemaha Agency, 1848–1856. R308.
_____. M234. St. Louis Superintendency, 1824–1841. R747-752.
_____. M234. Western Superintendency, 1832–1836. R921.
_____. M271. Letters Received by the Secretary of War Relating to Indian Affairs, 1817–1819. R2.
Record Group 107. M222. Letters Received by the Secretary of War, Unregistered Series, 1832–1833. R31.

Library of Congress

James Madison Papers, ser. 1, reel 22, Presidential Papers Microfilm.

Kansas State Historical Society, Topeka

George J. Remsburg Collection
History—Indians—General File

History—Indians—Kickapoo File
History—Indians—Potawatomi File

Missouri Historical Society Archives, St. Louis

Richard Graham Papers

Presbyterian Historical Society, Philadelphia

American Indian Correspondence, Collection of Missionary Letters, 1833-1893. Greenwood Press, Inc. Microfilm box 3.

Published Federal and State Government Documents

Senate Executive Documents

21st Cong., 2d sess., ser. 203, 1832
23rd Cong., 1st sess., ser. 247, 1833
25th Cong., 2d sess., ser. 314, 1837
26th Cong., 1st sess., ser. 354, 1839
27th Cong., 3d sess., ser. 413, 1842
28th Cong., 1st sess., ser. 431, 1843
32nd Cong., 1st sess., ser. 613, 1852
32nd Cong., 2d sess., ser. 658, 1852
36th Cong., 1st sess., ser. 1023, 1860

Carter, Clarence E., ed. *Territorial Papers of the United States.* Vol 17: *Illinois Territory, 1814-1818.* Washington, D.C.: Government Printing Office, 1950.
Edwards, Ninian. *The Edwards Papers; being a portion of a collection of the letters, papers, and manuscripts of Ninian Edwards.* Edited by E. B. Washburn. Chicago: Fergus Printing Co., 1884.
Green, Evarts B., and Alford, Charles W., eds. *Collections of the Illinois State Historical Library.* Vol. 4. Springfield: Illinois State Historical Library, 1909.
Harrison, William Henry. *Governor's Messages and Letters:*

Messages and Letters of William Henry Harrison, edited by Logan Esarey. Indianapolis: Indiana Historical Commission, 1922.

Kappler, Charles, comp. *Indian Affairs: Laws and Treaties*. Vol. 2. *Treaties*. Washington, D.C.: Government Printing Office, 1904.

Riker, Dorothy, and Thornbrough, Gayle, eds. *Messages and Papers Relating to the Administration of James Brown Ray, Governor of Indiana, 1825-1831*. Indianapolis: Indiana Historical Bureau, 1954.

Robertson, Nellie A., and Riker, Dorothy, eds. *The John Tipton Papers*. 3 vols. Indianapolis: Indiana Historical Bureau, 1942.

Newspapers

Illinois Intelligencer (Kaskaskia)
St. Joseph (Ind.) *Beacon*
St. Louis (Mo.) *Beacon*
Vandalia Whig and Illinois Intelligencer

Articles

Abel, Annie H. "The History of Events Resulting in Indian Consolidation West of the Mississippi." In *Annual Report of the American Historical Association for the Year 1906*, vol. 1, pp. 233-450.

Barnes, Lela, ed. "Journal of Isaac McCoy for the Exploring Expedition of 1828." *Kansas Historical Quarterly* 5 (August 1936): 227-277.

_____. "Journal of Isaac McCoy for the Exploring Expedition of 1830." *Kansas Historical Quarterly* 5 (November 1936): 339-377.

Barry, Louise, ed. "William Clark's Diary, May 1826-February 1831." *Kansas Historical Quarterly* 16 (February 1948): 1-36; (May 1948): 136-174; (August 1948): 274-305; (November 1948): 384-410.

Berryman, Jerome C. "A Circuit-Rider's Frontier Experiences." *Collections of the Kansas State Historical Society* 16 (1923-1925): 177-226.

Callender, Charles; Pope, Richard K.; and Pope, Susan M. "Kickapoo." In *Handbook of North American Indians*, vol. 15: *Northeast*, edited by Bruce G. Trigger, pp. 656-667. Washington, D.C.: Smithsonian Institution, 1978.

Custer, Milo. "Kannekuk or Keeanakuk: The Kickapoo Prophet." *Illinois State Historical Society Journal* 2 (April 1918): 48-56.

_____. "Masheena." *Transactions of the Illinois State Historical Society* (1911): 115-121.

Duignan, Peter. "Early Jesuit Missionaries: A Suggestion for Further Study." *American Anthropologist* 60 (August 1958): 725-732.

Dunbar, John, and Allis, Samuel. "Letters Concerning the Presbyterian Mission in the Pawnee Country, Near Bellevue, Neb., 1831-1849." *Collections of the Kansas State Historical Society* 14 (1918): 570-784.

Edmunds, R. David. "The Prairie Potawatomi Removal of 1833." *Indiana Magazine of History* 68 (September 1972): 240-253.

Ernst, Ferdinand. "Edwardsville, Vandalia, and the Sangamon Country." In *Prairie State: Impressions of Illinois, 1673-1967, By Travelers and Other Observers*, edited by Paul M. Angle, pp. 68-75. Chicago: University of Chicago Press, 1968.

Evans, David. "North American Indian Music." *Journal of American Folklore* 90 (July-September 1977): 364-371.

Forsyth, Thomas. "The Kickapoo Prophet." In *Indian Tribes of the Upper Mississippi Valley and Region of the Great Lakes*, edited by Emma Helen Blair. 2 vols. Cleveland, Ohio: Arthur H. Clark Co., 1911.

Garraghan, Gilbert J. "A Jesuit Westward Movement." *Mid-America* 18 (July 1936): 165-181.

_____. "The Kickapoo Mission." *St. Louis Catholic Historical Review* 4 (January-April 1922): 25-50.

_____. "Selected Letters from the Roux Correspondence." *Catholic Historical Review* 4 (April 1918): 84-100.

Hagan, William T. "Justifying Dispossession of the Indian: The Land Use Argument." In *American Indian Environments:*

Ecological Issues in Native American History, edited by Christopher Vecsey and Robert W. Venables, pp. 65-80. Syracuse, N.Y.: Syracuse University Press, 1980.

Herring, Joseph B. "Cultural and Economic Resilience among the Kickapoo Indians of the Southwest." *Great Plains Quarterly* 6 (Fall 1986): 263-275.

_____. "Kenekuk, the Kickapoo Prophet: Acculturation without Assimilation." *American Indian Quarterly* 9 (Summer 1985): 295-307. Republished in *American Indian Prophets: Religious Leaders and Revitalization Movements*, edited by Clifford E. Trafzer, pp. 57-69. Newcastle, Calif.: Sierra Oaks Publishing Co., 1986.

_____. "The Vermillion Kickapoos of Illinois: The Prophet Kenekuk's Peaceful Resistance to Indian Removal, 1819-1833." *Selected Papers in Illinois History, 1983* (Springfield: Illinois State Historical Society, 1985), pp. 28-38.

Howard, James H. "The Kenakuk Religion: An Early Nineteenth Century Revitalization Movement 140 Years Later." *Museum News* 26 (11/12, November/December 1965): 1-49.

Hoxie, Elizabeth F. "Harriet Livermore: 'Vixen and Devotee.' " *New England Quarterly* 18 (March 1945): 39-49.

Hubbard, Gurdon S. "A Kickapoo Sermon." *Illinois Monthly Magazine* 1 (October 1831): 473-476.

"Incidents of Frontier Life." *Journal of the Illinois State Historical Society* 32 (December 1939): 529.

Lonn, Ella. "Ripples of the Black Hawk War in Northern Indiana." *Indiana Magazine of History* 20 (September 1924): 288-307.

Lutz, J. J. "The Methodist Missions among the Indian Tribes in Kansas." *Transactions of the Kansas State Historical Society* 9 (1905/1906): 160-235.

McDermott, John Francis, ed. "Isaac McCoy's Second Exploring Trip in 1828." *Kansas Historical Quarterly* 13 (August 1945): 400-462.

McVicker, George C. "A Chapter in the Warfare against the Indians in Illinois during the Year of 1812." *Journal of the Illinois State Historical Society* 24 (July 1931): 342-343.

Miles, William. " 'Enamoured with Colonization': Isaac McCoy's

Plan of Indian Reform." *Kansas Historical Quarterly* 38 (Autumn 1972): 268-286.

Prucha, Francis Paul. "Andrew Jackson's Indian Policy: A Reassessment." *Journal of American History* 56 (December 1969): 527-539. Reprinted in *The Indian in American History*, edited by Francis Paul Prucha, pp. 67-74. Hinsdale, Ill.: Dryden Press, 1971.

_____. "Indian Removal and the Great American Desert." *Indiana Magazine of History* 59 (December 1963): 299-322.

_____. "Thomas L. McKenney and the New York Indian Board." *Mississippi Valley Historical Review* 48 (March 1962): 635-655.

Remsburg, George J. "Some Notes on the Kickapoo Indians." *Philatelic West* 36 (1907): 325-326.

Ronda, James P. "The European Indian: Jesuit Civilization Planning in New France." *Church History* 41 (September 1972): 385-395.

Schlesinger, Arthur M. "Casting the National Horoscope." *Proceedings of the American Antiquarian Society* 55 (April 1947): 53-94.

Schultz, George A. "Kennekuk, the Kickapoo Prophet." *Kansas History* 3 (Spring 1980): 38-46.

Thomas, Peter A. "Contrastive Subsistence Strategies and Land Use as Factors for Understanding Indian-White Relations in New England." *Ethnohistory* 23 (Winter 1976): 1-18.

Van Quickenborne, Charles F. "Relation d'un voyage fait chez les tribus indiennes situées à l'ouest du Missouri." *Annales de la propagation de la foi* 9 (September 1836): 99-101.

Voget, Fred W. "The American Indian in Transition: Reformation and Accommodation." *American Anthropologist* 58 (April 1956): 249-263.

Wallace, Anthony F. C. "Revitalization Movements." *American Anthropologist* 58 (April 1956): 249-263.

Washburn, Wilcomb E. "Indian Removal Policy: Administrative, Historical and Moral Criteria for Judging Its Success or Failure." *Ethnohistory* 12 (Summer 1965): 274-278.

_____. "The Moral and Legal Justification for Dispossessing the Indians." In *Seventeenth Century America: Essays in Colonial*

History, edited by James Morton Smith, pp. 15–32. New York: W. W. Norton & Co., Inc., 1972.

Wilmeth, Roscoe. "Kansa Village Locations in Light of Isaac McCoy's 1828 Journal." *Kansas Historical Quarterly* 26 (Summer 1960): 152–157.

Young, Mary E. "Indian Removal and Land Allotment: The Civilized Tribes and Jacksonian Justice." *American Historical Review* 64 (October 1958): 31–45.

Books

Adams, John Quincy. *Memoirs of John Quincy Adams, Comprising Portions of His Diary from 1795 to 1848*, edited by Charles Francis Adams. 12 vols. Freeport, N.Y.: Books for Libraries Press, 1969.

Arese, Count Francesco. *A Trip to the Prairies and in the Interior of North America [1837–1838]*. New York: Cooper Square Publishers, 1975.

Barry, Louise. *The Beginning of the West: Annals of the Kansas Gateway to the American West, 1540–1854*. Topeka: Kansas State Historical Society, 1972.

Beckwith, H. W., and Burnham, J. H. *An Ancient Indian Fort: Some Accounts of Its History, with an Outline of the Works*. Bloomington, Ill.: Pantagraph Printing Establishment, 1881.

Berkhofer, Robert F., Jr. *Salvation and the Savage: An Analysis of Protestant Missions and American Indian Response, 1787–1862*. New York: Atheneum, 1976.

Blair, Emma Helen, ed. *The Indian Tribes of the Upper Mississippi Valley and Region of the Great Lakes*. 2 Vols. Cleveland: Arthur H. Clark Co., 1911.

Bowden, Henry Warner. *American Indians and Christian Missions: Studies in Cultural Conflict*. Chicago: University of Chicago Press, 1981.

Callan, Louise. *Philippine Duchesne: Frontier Missionary of the Sacred Heart, 1769–1852*. Westminster, Md.: Newman Press, 1957.

Catlin, George. *Letters and Notes on the Manners, Customs, and Conditions of the North American Indians*. 2 vols. New York: Dover Publications, Inc., 1973.

Clifton, James A. *The Prairie People: Continuity and Change in Potawatomi Indian Culture, 1665–1965*. Lawrence: Regents Press of Kansas, 1977.

De Smet, Pierre Jean. *Life, Letters, and Travels of Father Pierre-Jean De Smet, S.J., 1801–1873, Missionary Labors and Adventures among the Wild Tribes of the North American Indians, Embracing Minute Descriptions of Their Manners, Customs, Games, Modes of Warfare and Torture, Legends, Traditions, etc.* Edited by Hiram M. Chittenden and Alfred T. Richardson. New York: Francis P. Harper, 1905; reprint, New York: Kraus Reprint Co., 1969.

Duir, E. *The Good Old Times in McLean County, Illinois*. Illinois: McKnight & McKnight Publishing Co., 1968.

Edmunds, R. David. *The Potawatomis: Keepers of the Fire*. Norman: University of Oklahoma Press, 1978.

_____. *Tecumseh and the Quest for Indian Leadership*. Boston: Little, Brown and Co., 1984.

_____. *The Shawnee Prophet*. Lincoln: University of Nebraska Press, 1983.

Edwards, Ninian W. *History of Illinois from 1778 to 1833; and Life and Times of Ninian Edwards*. Springfield: Illinois State Journal Co., 1870; reprint, Arno Press, 1975.

Foreman, Grant. *The Last Trek of the Indians*. Chicago: University of Chicago Press, 1946.

Garraghan, Gilbert J. *Catholic Beginnings in Kansas City, Missouri: An Historical Sketch*. Chicago: Loyola University Press, 1920.

_____. *The Jesuits of the Middle United States*. 3 vols. New York: America Press, 1938.

Gates, Paul Wallace. *Fifty Million Acres: Conflicts over Kansas Land Policy, 1854–1890*. Ithaca, N.Y.: Cornell University Press, 1954.

Gibson, Arrell M. *The Kickapoos: Lords of the Middle Border*. Norman: University of Oklahoma Press, 1963.

Hagan, William T. *The Sac and Fox Indians.* Norman: University of Oklahoma Press, 1958.

Hoad, Louise Green. *Kickapoo Indian Trails.* Caldwell, Idaho: Caxton Printers, Ltd., 1946.

Hoffman, Charles F. *A Winter in the West, by a New Yorker.* New York: Harper & Brothers, 1835.

Horsman, Reginald. *The Origins of Indian Removal, 1815-1824.* East Lansing: Michigan State University Press, 1970.

Irving, John Treat. *Indian Sketches, Taken during an Expedition to the Pawnee Tribes (1833).* Edited by John Francis McDermott. Norman: University of Oklahoma Press, 1955.

Josephy, Alvin M., Jr. *The Patriot Chiefs: A Chronicle of American Indian Resistance.* New York: Viking Press, 1961.

Livermore, Harriet. *The Harp of Israel to Meet the Loud Echo in the Wilds of America.* Philadelphia: J. Rakestraw, 1835.

———. *A Letter to John Ross, the Principle Chief of the Cherokee Nation.* Philadelphia: The Author, 1838.

———. *Millennial Tidings.* Philadelphia: The Author, 1839.

———. *A Narration of Religious Experience, in Twelve Letters.* 2 Vols. Concord, N.H.: Printed by Jacob Moore for the Author, 1826.

Livermore, S. T. *Harriet Livermore the "Pilgrim Stranger."* Hartford, Conn.: Lockwood & Brainard Co., 1884.

McCord, Shirley S., ed. *Travel Accounts of Indiana, 1679-1961: A Collection of Observations by Wayfaring Foreigners, Itinerants, and Peripatetic Hoosiers.* Bloomington: Indiana Historical Bureau, 1970.

McCoy, Isaac. *History of Baptist Indian Missions.* Washington, D.C.: W. M. Morrison; and New York: H. & S. Raynor, 1840.

Miner, H. Craig, and Unrau, William E. *The End of Indian Kansas: A Study of Cultural Revolution, 1854-1871.* Lawrence: Regents Press of Kansas, 1978.

Mooney, James. *The Ghost-Dance Religion and Wounded Knee.* New York: Dover Publications, 1973.

Moore, Virginia. *The Madisons: A Biography.* New York: McGraw-Hill Book Co., 1979.

Murray, Charles Augustus. *Travels in North America during the*

Years 1834, 1835, and 1836, Including a Summer Residence with the Pawnee Tribe of Indians. . . . 2 vols. London: Richard Bentley, 1839.

Prucha, Francis Paul. *American Indian Policy in the Formative Years: The Indian Trade and Intercourse Acts, 1790–1834*. Lincoln: University of Nebraska Press, 1973.

Rogin, Michael Paul. *Fathers and Children: Andrew Jackson and the Subjugation of the American Indian*. New York: Vantage Books, 1976.

Satz, Ronald N. *American Indian Policy in the Jacksonian Era*. Lincoln: University of Nebraska Press, 1975.

Schultz, George A. *An Indian Canaan: Isaac McCoy and the Vision of an Indian State*. Norman: University of Oklahoma Press, 1972.

Sheehan, Bernard W. *Seeds of Extinction: Jeffersonian Philanthropy and the American Indian*. New York: W. W. Norton & Co., Inc., 1974.

Spicer, Edward H. *Cycles of Conquest: The Impact of Spain, Mexico, and the United States on the Indians of the Southwest, 1533–1960*. Tucson: University of Arizona Press, 1962.

Steffen, Jerome O. *William Clark: Jeffersonian Man on the Frontier*. Norman: University of Oklahoma Press, 1977.

Sweet, William W. *Religion on the American Frontier, 1783–1840*. Vol. 4: *The Methodists: A Collection of Source Materials*. New York: Cooper Square Publishers, 1964.

Thomas, David. *Travels through the Western Country in the Summer of 1816*. Darien, Conn.: Hafner Publishing Co., 1970.

Trafzer, Clifford E., ed. *American Indian Prophets: Religious Leaders and Revitalization Movements*. Newcastle, Calif.: Sierra Oaks Publishing Co., 1986.

Trennert, Robert A., Jr. *Alternative to Extinction: Federal Indian Policy and the Beginnings of the Reservation System, 1846–1851*. Philadelphia: Temple University Press, 1975.

Unrau, William E. *The Emigrant Indians of Kansas: A Critical Bibliography*. Bloomington: Indiana University Press, 1979.

Van Every, Dale. *Disinherited: The Lost Birthright of the American Indian*. New York: Avon Books, 1966.

Viola, Herman J. *Thomas L. McKenney: Architect of America's Early Indian Policy, 1816-1830.* Chicago: Swallow Press, 1974.

Wallace, Anthony F. C. *Prelude to Disaster: The Course of Indian-White Relations Which Led to the Black Hawk War of 1832.* Springfield: Illinois State Historical Library, 1970.

Whittier, John Greenleaf. *The Letters of John Greenleaf Whittier.* Vol. 3: *1861-1892.* Edited by John B. Pickard. Cambridge, Mass.: Belknap Press of Harvard University Press, 1975.

Index

169